BIBLE BASICS
for Catholics

"If you're looking for the single best introduction to the Bible, this is it. Dr. Bergsma's clarity, depth, and faithfulness make *Bible Basics for Catholics* an indispensable guide for anyone who wants to understand the story of scripture."

Fr. Mike Schmitz
Host of the *Bible in a Year* podcast

"It would be worth it to go back to college just to learn from a master teacher such as John Bergsma. Bergsma leads us by way of history and imagination to the Holy Land, and to times long past, and we meet the most fascinating people who ever lived: Abraham, Moses, David, and Jesus. We can do all this because of Bergsma's rare gifts. This book can change lives."

Mike Aquilina
Author, journalist, and executive vice president
of the St. Paul Center for Biblical Theology

"We simply can't say that studying the Old Testament is intimidating anymore, not when there is the work of John Bergsma to help us through the door. *Bible Basics for Catholics* is a wonderful guide to begin the journey, not only for the individual but also for the entire family. It seems like a simple presentation, but it is so packed with important fundamental elements of Sacred Scripture that you hardly realize that you've mastered the 'heavy' things. Instead, you come away more aware and deeply appreciative of the 'family' history we've been given."

Kris McGregor
Founder and executive director of Discerning Hearts

"Even though this is a basic, nonintimidating overview of the Bible, John Bergsma is not afraid to deepen our appreciation of scripture by occasionally introducing some important technical terms and Hebrew and Greek words, always explaining them thoroughly and understandably."

National Catholic Register

"You're a Catholic. You would like to study the Bible, but you're not sure where to start. You'd love to take a class, but you're busy. Let award-winning teacher John Bergsma guide you through a high-energy and entertaining walk through the Bible, illustrated with his own charming drawings. This book is so fresh, engaging, and truly instructive that you will find yourself smiling as you read it, and you'll be amazed at what you retain."

Elizabeth Scalia
Catholic author, blogger, and editor at large

"As a homeschooling mom trying to pass on the beauty of our Catholic faith to my kids, I have been incredibly blessed by *Bible Basics for Catholics*. John Bergsma has a way of making scripture come alive—clear, engaging, and faithful to Church teaching. I love how he walks through the big story of salvation, from the Garden of Eden all the way to Jesus, in a way that's easy to understand but never watered down. This expanded edition, with study questions and videos, makes it even easier to share with my family and our parish group. I've learned so much myself, and I know others will too."

Jackie Angel
Author of *Memorize Scripture*

"John Bergsma brings his biblical scholarship, pastoral heart, and gift for teaching together in this charming, easy-to-use overview of salvation history. Catechists, teachers, and pastoral ministers will find this an inestimable resource, both for their own reference and for shepherding those under their care. Perfect for use in religious education settings, in small-group study, and as an undergraduate course text. Highly recommended."

Edward Sri
Theologian, author, speaker, and senior vice president of apostolic outreach for FOCUS

EXPANDED EDITION

BIBLE BASICS for Catholics

A New Picture of Salvation History

John Bergsma

Ave Maria Press AVE Notre Dame, Indiana

Unless otherwise indicated, Scripture quotations are from the *Revised Standard Version Bible,* copyright © 1952 and 1965 by the Division of Christian Education of the National Council of Churches of Christ in the USA. Used by permission. All rights reserved.

Excerpts from *Bible Basics for Catholics Discussion Guide* by Maria Morera Johnson, copyright © 2019 by Ave Maria Press.

Nihil Obstat: Reverend Monsignor Michael Heintz, PhD
Censor librorum
Imprimatur: Most Reverend Kevin C. Rhoades
Bishop of Fort Wayne–South Bend
December 6, 2011

Foreword © 2025 by Scott Hahn

© 2012, 2015 by John Bergsma

All rights reserved. No part of this book may be used or reproduced in any manner whatsoever, except in the case of reprints in the context of reviews, without written permission from Ave Maria Press®, Inc., P.O. Box 428, Notre Dame, IN 46556, 1-800-282-1865.

Founded in 1865, Ave Maria Press is a ministry of the Congregation of Holy Cross, United States Province.

www.avemariapress.com

Paperback: ISBN-13 978-1-64680-340-8

E-book: ISBN-13 978-1-64680-341-5

Special Edition product number: 30019

Cover design by Samantha Watson.

Text design by Andy Wagoner and Samantha Watson.

Illustrations rendered by K. Hornyak Bonelli.

Printed and bound in the United States of America.

Library of Congress Cataloging-in-Publication Data is available.

Contents

Foreword by Scott Hahn ix

How to Use This Book as a Self-Study xi

How to Use This Book in a Small
    Group xiii

Introduction 1

One Setting the Son in the Garden
The Covenant with Adam 9

Two Washing Up and Starting Over
The Covenant with Noah 37

Three A New Hope
The Covenant with Abraham 51

Four God's Laws, Israel's Flaws
The Covenant through Moses 73

Five Once and Future King
The Covenant of David 103

Six Stormy Today, Sonny Tomorrow
The New Covenant in the Prophets 125

Seven The Grand Finale
   The Eucharistic Covenant 151

Eight Covenant Consummation
   The Wedding Feast of the Lamb 189

A Last Word 209

Notes 213

Suggestions for Further Reading 237

Foreword

I was honored, back in 2012, to write the foreword for the first edition of this book—honored because I believed *Bible Basics for Catholics* would become an instant classic. On my first reading I recognized that this was a book written with breadth, clarity, and accessibility. It was the work of a master scholar, a master teacher, and a master writer.

And wasn't I right? *Bible Basics for Catholics* immediately became something of a gold standard for Catholic biblical instruction at an introductory level. This is my field, so I know. I've used it in my own classes and teaching, and many other teachers I know have taken to it immediately.

What's truly remarkable is that it is still used—more and more widely—in high schools, colleges, parishes, and private studies. Rare is the text that's right for any two of those audiences, never mind all of them. But the qualities I mentioned—breadth, clarity, and accessibility—made it the right choice for every situation.

The book has held up for more than a dozen years. Already, students who cut their teeth on the first edition have gone on in their studies and are using it in their own classrooms and parishes.

Thus, I feel honored, once again, to speak on behalf of this book, now revised, now expanded, now still more useful than it was. This new edition equips anyone looking to dive deeper into a Catholic reading of scripture. The chapter-by-chapter self-study questions make this new edition perfect for at-home study (such as in a homeschool or for a motivated forever-learner), and the small-group guides provide everything readers need to run a small-group meeting with their communities. No more searching online for how to adapt the material for these settings. Everything is now in the book proper.

In closing, I want to commend this book and its author to a new generation of students and readers. Indeed, I have known the author for a quarter of a century now. Dr. Bergsma is my close friend and neighbor, my colleague, and a very gifted writer and teacher to tens of thousands of students—including my own children and now my grandchildren.

Scott Hahn

How to Use This Book as a Self-Study

Each chapter closes with a lesson to help the reader study what they've just read. The lessons lend themselves well to reviewing alongside a one-semester theology course in a Catholic high school. *Bible Basics for Catholics* works particularly well in combination with an introductory course on salvation history (e.g., Course I, The Revelation of Jesus Christ in Scripture, of the USCCB Framework), with a course on the Bible (e.g., Old Testament; New Testament; or Elective A, Sacred Scripture, of the USCCB Framework), or with any other introductory course on the Catholic faith. The book can be taught over eight or four weeks:

- **Eight weeks.** Read one chapter per week. Complete some or all of the activities suggested in the chapter's lesson. *Suggestion:* Reserve one day per week for focused study.
- **Four weeks.** Read two chapters per week. Complete some or all of the activities suggested in each chapter's lesson. *Suggestion:* Reserve two days per week for focused study.

Bible Basics for Catholics also can be used with a campus ministry Bible study, a Confirmation preparation class, or a parish's youth catechetical program.

How to Use the Self-Study Elements

Each lesson includes three sections that help support the chapter's content. Reading should be completed before turning to the lessons. Use a notebook to record your answers and to draw your own sketches.

Background

The background material is intended to summarize the main point of the chapter. Read the paragraph to refresh and supplement your understanding of the material.

Reading Comprehension

The reading comprehension questions help you determine whether you have closely read the chapter. All of the answers are found in that lesson's chapter. These can be worked on immediately after you've read the chapter or a few days later to see how much you have retained.

Writing Assignment

The writing assignment—usually not more than four or five paragraphs in length—is drawn from the chapter text, a separate article or link, or a scripture passage. Some of the assignments involve drawing sketches like the ones in the book.

How to Use This Book in a Small Group

Whether you're reading *Bible Basics for Catholics* with a group from your parish, in your regular small group or book club, or on your own, the small-group guide at the end of each chapter is designed to help you get the most out of your reading. The questions are meant to be read and discussed after each chapter. If you're reading this on your own, take time after each chapter to pray and reflect on these questions. If this book is being read by a group, leaders can look to the following instructions.

Instructions for Small-Group Leaders

The small-group guides are designed to cover eight one- to two-hour meetings, plus a ninth closing session, but this schedule can be adjusted to meet the needs of the group. If a group is being created specifically to discuss this book, you might find it helpful to have a half-hour introductory session in which group members can meet each other and books can be handed out prior to the first meeting for discussion. Consider recommending that readers use journals to prepare for each week's session and to reflect on the group discussion.

Introduction

You ought to know the Bible better than you do, and you probably feel vaguely guilty that you don't. Come on, admit it. You know it's true. I know it's true. Most of us Catholics who show up for Mass week after week have heard a bunch of homilies or shows on EWTN or talks on CD urging us to get to know the scriptures better. Most of us have heard someone quote one of the popes saying, "The scriptures are letters from our loving Father" or St. Jerome's famous line that "ignorance of scripture is ignorance of Christ."

Do you know how those quotes have made us feel? Ignorant. And maybe guilty. Guilty that we don't really read the Bible that much.

Some of us have tried. We've made resolutions to read the whole Bible through in a year or follow some other plan. At best we get through Genesis, maybe Exodus, but once we hit all the laws and sacrifices of Leviticus, it's game over.

Getting more education doesn't necessarily help. You sign up for a Bible class at your parish or take one at the university. The teacher spends the whole time explaining that nothing was actually written by the apostle or prophet whose name is on the book—it was all composed much later by someone named "P" or "Q" and their "community"—and you wind up more confused about the Bible than ever.

I can relate to that feeling. I grew up in a home where we *did* try to read the Bible a lot. No, I wasn't Catholic—I became one later in life, but that's a different story. Anyway, my mom started me reading the Bible through in a year when I was about twelve. I didn't keep it up consistently, but I did manage to slog through most of it over a number of years—not understanding everything, but here and there hitting some interesting stories and teachings.

Later in life I started to get more interested in the Bible, so I took a couple of graduate programs in scripture. In fact, I took so many courses in scripture that after about twelve years of schooling *after* my high school graduation, I found myself with a master's degree and a PhD in scripture. But strangely, I still wasn't sure I understood how it all fit together much better than when I was twelve.

To be sure, I had learned a lot in graduate school about the languages scripture was written in; a lot about what other people had said about the Bible over the past two thousand years; and a wide assortment of theories about what "really happened" at different points in the Bible and who "really" wrote it and why. But I didn't get too much of what the Bible was "all about." I understood that, in the end, the Bible as Christians understand it focuses ultimately on Jesus. But beyond that, I still didn't see how it fit together as one book from God.

It was only in the years after I finished my PhD in scripture, when I was forced to get ready to teach Bible to college freshmen, that I began to see the unity of the Bible through the concept of the covenant. This was nothing I came up with myself: it was good friends (one in particular), good books, and the Church's liturgy that helped me to see it.

What I want to share with you in this book is the basic, overall "big picture" of the Bible I wish I myself had started with when I first began to read the Bible seriously about thirty years ago. I feel that it took me twelve years of schooling after high school just to discover square one—almost by accident. My hope is that you will not have to wait twelve years to get to square one.

If you can hang with me for a few short chapters, I think the Bible's big picture will begin to make more sense for you, too. Plus, you'll pick up some great stick-figure drawings along the way! I will use what we shall very loosely call "art" in order to help make some key points—very useful for the next time you play Pictionary. These drawings are intended to teach the Bible's "covenants" by focusing on a sequence of "mediators on mountains."

It All Starts with Covenant

I'm going to try to keep the big words and technical jargon to a minimum. That's partly because I don't think it's all that helpful or necessary. The Apostle John wrote the world's best-selling and most influential book ever—the Gospel of John—using a third- or fourth-grade vocabulary. Yet what he was able to say with such simple words has continued to amaze the world ever since! However, there are a few terms we probably ought to discuss.

The first is "covenant." We've all heard this word in Mass, although we may not have paid much attention to it. One of the Eucharistic Prayers (the prayers the priest leads us in during the second half of Mass) includes a line you may remember as follows: "Again and again you offered a covenant to man, and through the prophets taught him to hope for salvation." The newer translation has the same meaning: "Time and again you offered them [humanity] covenants and through the prophets taught them to look forward to salvation." That little line is a way of summarizing almost the whole message of the Bible. This little book in your hands is really just a small explanation of that one line.

The other, more famous place we hear "covenant" is when the priest consecrates the cup at Mass. For years we heard, "This is the cup of my blood, the blood of the new and everlasting covenant." The new translation reads, "This is the chalice of my Blood, the Blood of the new and eternal covenant."

St. John Paul II, whom many call "John Paul the Great," often called the Eucharist the "Source and Summit of the Christian life." And in the Mass, the Eucharist is called a "covenant." Therefore, covenant must be a Big Deal. And it is.

But what is a "covenant"?

Some people will say that a covenant is like a contract, except that you exchange persons, not property. That's correct, so far as it goes. Others will say that a covenant is *a legal way to make someone part of your family*—obviously, someone who wasn't part of your family before. That's a very useful definition for our purposes.

Two excellent examples of a covenant are adoption and marriage. In the case of adoption, at least in the ancient world, you would take a child unrelated to you before the priests, village elders, or some other official and swear solemn oaths that the child was now yours. Then you went home with a new son or daughter. In the case of marriage, to this day, we typically stand before a priest, minister, or—at the very least—a judge and swear solemn oaths to each other. Two people enter the building as John White and Jane Brown, and leave husband and wife. Two "strangers" have become family by making a covenant. So, when the priest prays at Mass, "Time and again you offered them covenants," it means, "God has repeatedly tried to make us his family."

Marriage is perhaps not as popular a thing as it used to be a generation ago. People put it off longer and longer, if they ever get around to it at all. Relationships are casual—guys and girls "hook up" for a while and then "unhook," I suppose, and move on to someone else. Singles live in dread of the C word: "Commitment."

God, on the other hand, believes in marriage and family. The relationship he seeks with all of us, and each one of us personally, is no casual affair, no on-again, off-again dating game. The covenant relationship he wants with us is a marriage: chocolate and flowers, big diamond ring, "till death do us part," house in the suburbs, and pitter patter of little feet. Yes, God is interested in children—they complete a family. The Bible says as much: "What does He desire? Godly children" (Mal 2:15).

God is all about commitment and love that lasts "till death do us part" and beyond, because not even death parts us from God. All that is packed into the little word "covenant."

Mediator

Besides "covenant," there's one other somewhat technical term we need to talk about: "mediator." It often happened in ancient times that folks wanted to make covenants that involved more than just two people. For example, perhaps a king wanted to let a group of foreigners into his "family" (which basically meant into his kingdom); he would then make a covenant with them. Usually, one person would step forward to represent the group with whom the covenant was made—that person was the "mediator."

So we can talk about "covenant mediators," by which we mean: persons who represent groups of people involved in a covenant. In the Bible, there are a number of important covenant mediators. The most significant ones are Adam, Noah, Abraham, Moses, David, and Jesus. Each of them entered into a covenant with God, and each of them represented a group of people who entered into God's covenant through them.

Mountain

The last term we need to define is "mountain." Well, actually, we don't need to define it because everyone knows what a mountain is except for folks from mostly flat places like Illinois, Louisiana, or Florida. But I digress. Anyway, we do need to talk about mountains and why they are significant.

In the course of the Bible, God makes at least six major covenants with the men I mentioned above: Adam, Noah, Abraham, Moses, David, and Jesus. Years ago, when I was first teaching the Bible's story line—which we call "salvation history"—I was looking for ways to simplify and visualize this pattern of covenants. Looking for what they all had in common, I noticed that each of the six covenants *was made on a mountaintop,* that is, the ritual or ceremony for each took place on top of a mountain.

That can hardly be an accident. There must be something about mountains that makes them suitable for meeting God. What might that be?

An old and wise priest pointed out to me some years ago that mountains make you feel closer to God. There are a couple of reasons for this: First of all, mountain peaks tend to be lonely places. Without all the usual people and business around, it's easier to focus on basic reality: yourself and God.

Second, mountain peaks help a person to get a "God's-eye" view of things. When viewed from a mountaintop, the farm you might live on, which seemed so enormous when you were in the valley, is now the size of a postage stamp. Now you can see it is only one of dozens or even hundreds of farms stretching out in all directions to the horizon. Things that looked intimidating down below now look small, and you can see they are part of a much bigger pattern not visible before.

From a mountaintop, (1) you are more or less alone with God; (2) you can see much more; (3) it all looks smaller; and (4) you can see everything *in context,* that is, together with its surroundings. Maybe these are some reasons people feel closer to God on top of a mountain and describe strong religious feelings as "mountaintop experiences."

You may wish to read and discuss this book together with other friends or with a parish or school group. If so, you will find the small-group guides at the end of each chapter helpful in guiding discussion.

On with the Show

That's it for preliminaries. In what follows, we're going to take a whirlwind tour of the Bible, emphasizing five "mountaintop" experiences with the mediators Adam, Noah, Abraham, Moses, and David. Then we'll talk about the prophets who predicted a "New Covenant" on a new mountaintop, the heavenly Mount Zion. We'll see that what the prophets predicted came true, sometimes in an unexpected way, through the Eucharistic Covenant established by Jesus in the gospels. Finally, we'll conclude with a brief vision of the beauty that awaits us at the end of time: the wedding covenant of the "Bride" and the "Lamb" in the Book of Revelation.

ONE
SETTING THE SON IN THE GARDEN
The Covenant with Adam

Suggested Reading: Genesis 1-2

What Is the Meaning of Life?

What is the meaning of life? Isn't that the question everyone wants answered?

When I was a teenager, my friends and I were hilariously entertained by Douglas Adams's book series *The Hitchhiker's Guide to the Galaxy*. The main character in that series, Arthur Dent, eventually discovers that the meaning of life is "42." The author Adams was being cynical—a staunch atheist, he didn't think there *was* any meaning to life. To ascribe a random number to the question was his clever way of making the point. At the time, I thought Adams's books were funny because—as a Christian—I didn't take them seriously. Had I *really* thought there was no better answer to the meaning of life than "42," it wouldn't have been funny. It would've been depressing.

The search for meaning in life is related to the search for our origins. "Why are we here?" is tied up with "Where did we come from?" People have always been fascinated with genealogies—at least with their own. I remember the amazement I felt when my oldest uncle gave my family a copy of the Bergsma genealogy he had constructed—a narrow roll of paper several feet in length, tracing our ancestors back to strange-named and long-forgotten Dutch farmers and merchants of the 1700s. There was even a hint that we might have some blood in common with the Dutch royal family.

Nowadays, the internet boasts several sites that will help you trace your ancestry, and they do brisk business. Why? Why do people even care who their forefathers and foremothers were?

Somehow, knowing where we came from helps us figure out where we ought to go. Knowing one's ancestors gives meaning to one's life here and now.

Maybe that's why the Bible devotes a fair amount of space telling us about our first father, Adam, and his wife, our first mother, Eve. The Bible is pretty specific about the reasons Adam was made and what his role in the universe was to be. Moreover, Adam was and is a model for all of us. The purpose (or meaning) of his life remains the purpose of each of our lives.

Before we take a look at the purpose (or *purposes*) of Adam's life, bear with me for a moment while we sketch in some background. After all, Adam wasn't the first thing God created.

The Creation Week: Building a Temple

Everyone knows about the "six days of creation" described in the book of Genesis. Usually the subject comes up nowadays when people discuss "Creationism" versus "Darwinism," or when local or statewide school boards have to decide on science texts and standards for the public schools. People naturally want to ask, "Are these six days literal?" "Is the earth really so young?" "How does this story square with the Big Bang and evolution?"

Those are all good questions, but we need to put them on the back burner for the moment because those are not the primary questions the writer of Genesis wanted to answer. Instead, the inspired author wanted to teach us something about the purpose for which God made the world in the first place. The Bible begins with a summary statement: "In the beginning God created the heavens and the earth" (Gn 1:1). Then it gets into the specifics of how God went about it.

The next verse says, "And the earth was formless and void, and darkness was over the face of the waters" (Gn 1:2). The picture here is of a world—or universe—that exists, but is not finished yet. It has two problems: it is "formless" and "void."

Genesis was written in Hebrew, and in Hebrew the words "formless and void" make the fun phrase "tohu wabohu"—it is a rhyming phrase that describes a situation of chaos, like our phrase "higgledy-piggledy." More specifically, "tohu" means "formless," that is, "unformed" or "unshaped." "Bohu," on the other hand, means "void" or "empty."

So, God calls the cosmos into existence, but it has two "problems": it is unformed and empty. It needs to be formed and filled. That is what God sets out to do in the following six days.

It's not too hard to draw this out. Drawing helps us remember things and makes it easier to explain it to others, like your kids, a catechism class, or even your spouse. (By the way, when you draw the sketches in this book yourself, it's best to use something that erases, because sometimes the figures change as they're being filled out.)

To illustrate the days of creation, let's draw a tall box and divide it into six squares. Make the box as big as you can because we'll need to draw inside each square:

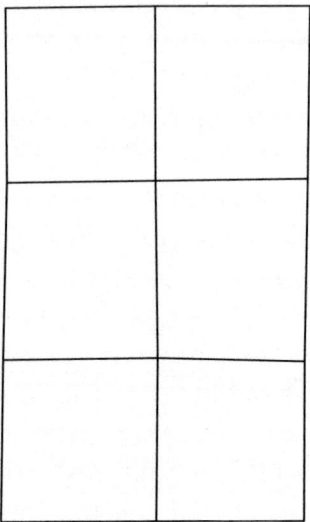

Now number the squares one through six starting in the bottom left-hand corner, like so:

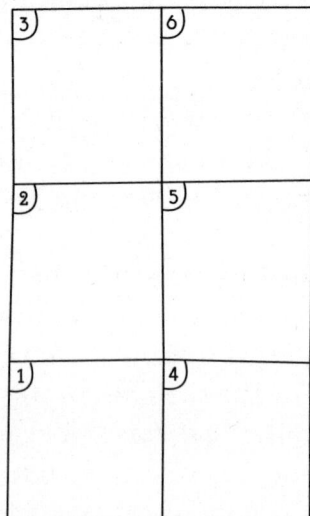

The Covenant with Adam

Now, the squares on the left-hand side (boxes 1–3) represent the first three days of creation, in which God addresses the "problem" of formlessness. He is going to form and shape the creation, starting on the first day, when he creates the light and the darkness, calling the one "day" and the other "night."

This is easy to illustrate. Just cut square one in half diagonally. Fill in the bottom half with the side of your pencil.

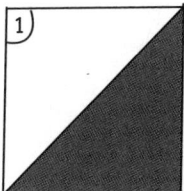

There. You have just illustrated the first day, the creation of light and dark, day and night. This is the creation of "Time," so write the word "Time" to the side of your diagram like so:

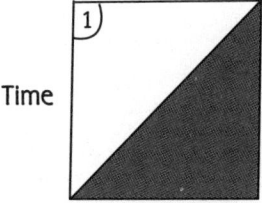

On the second day, God creates the great expanses of space, the skies, and the seas. These are not difficult to sketch. For the sea, make a squiggly line like so:

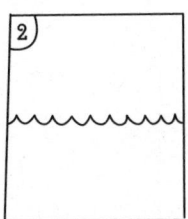

And for the sky, a cloud or two will work:

God has now formed "Space," so write "Space" to the side like so:

On the third day, God creates the dry land and the vegetation. Let's make an island in the "sea" with a simple curve.

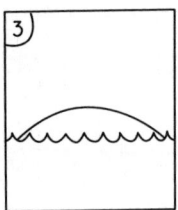

A tree and a few blades of grass will represent the vegetation.

Let's write "Habitat" to the side. The dry land and vegetation will provide a home for animals and eventually for humans.

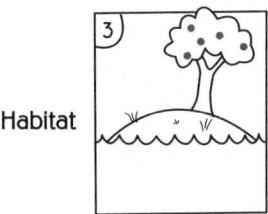

At the end of the three days, God has solved the issue of "formlessness." The cosmos is formed, but it remains "bohu" or "empty." The next three days (days 4–6) address this issue.

First, the realm of "Time"—the day and night—is filled with inhabitants: the sun, moon, and stars. These are set in place to mark the passage of time and to indicate the "seasons," in Hebrew *mo'ed* ("Moe-AID"), which means specifically "liturgical seasons." In other words, the sun, moon, and stars mark the passage of time so people on earth will know when to worship. The sun and moon are there to tell you when to go to Mass!

The sun can be a simple circle with some radiating lines:

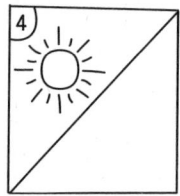

The moon is a basic crescent, and the stars are easy enough to draw:

The realm of "Time" is now inhabited.

On the fifth day, God moves on to filling the great spaces with the birds and the fish. A few well-placed curves can serve as fish and fowl:

Just the "Habitat" remains now. On the sixth day, God makes the animals and man (Adam). For the animals, do the best you can. I like to make a snake and a giraffe. For Adam, a stick figure will do:

The Covenant with Adam

Creation is almost complete—except for the climax, the "roof" on the whole building. That's the seventh day, the Sabbath, the day of rest and worship. Let's mark that by putting a roof on top:

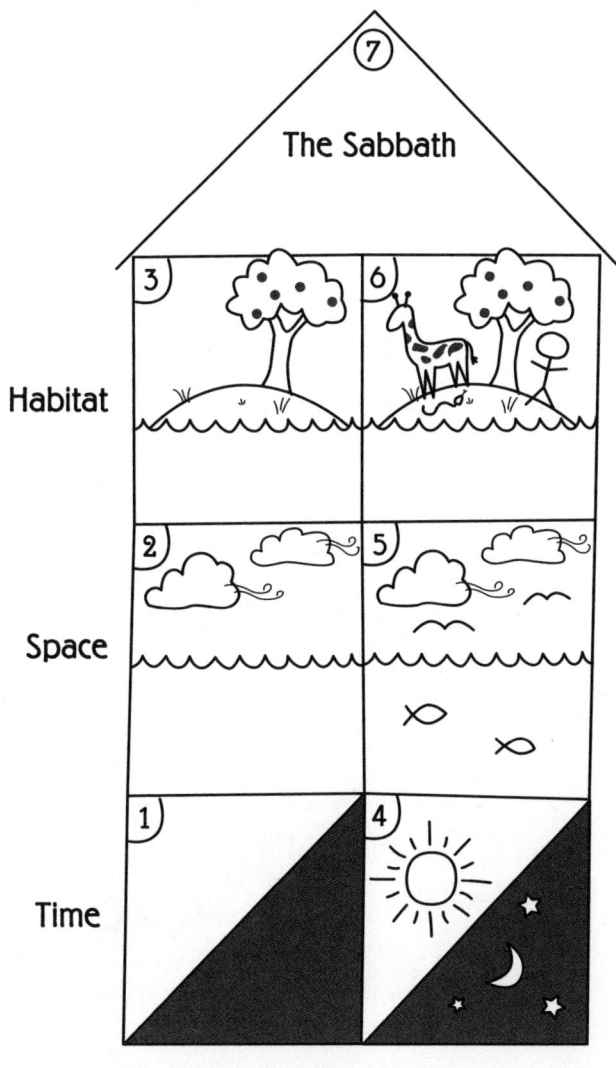

The structure we've been building is a temple. As Christians, we mark a house of worship with a cross, so if you want to put a steeple and cross on the top, go ahead:

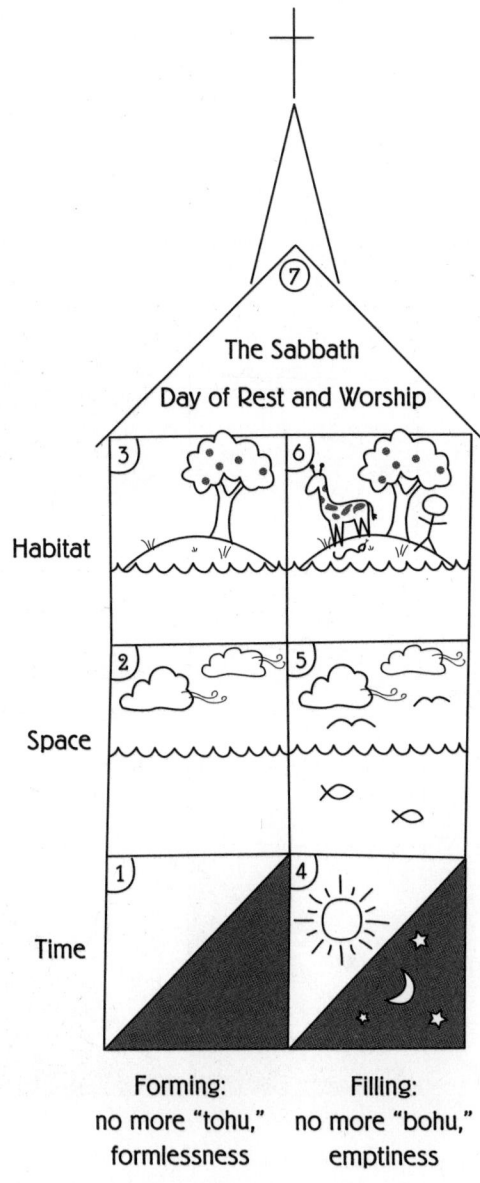

The Covenant with Adam

Congratulations! You've just drawn a picture of the temple-universe that God built in seven days. You may ask, how do we know this "building" of creation is a temple? Here are some reasons:

1. The language of creation resembles the language of Moses building the Tabernacle in the wilderness. (Compare Genesis 2:1–3 with Exodus 39:32, 42–43.)
2. Some scriptures speak of the creation as a temple (Ps 78:69; Ps 148).
3. In other ancient writings from about the same time as Genesis, it is clear that people considered the whole universe a kind of temple for worship of God (or the gods). It was a common idea in ancient times.

✣ ✣ ✣

So, now we can return to asking our questions about the creation of Adam. What was the purpose of his life? The first thing the Bible tells us about Adam is that he was created "in the image and likeness of God." What does that mean? If we fast-forward to Genesis 5:3, we get a clue as to what it means to be "made in the image and likeness." In Genesis 5:3 we read, "When Adam had lived a hundred and thirty years, he became the father of a son in his own *likeness*, after his *image*, and named him Seth." So what does "image and likeness" mean? It means *to be a son*. The fancy theological term is *divine filiation (FIL-ee-AY-shun)*—we're talking about being a child of God.

That's the first thing we need to know about Adam. He was the son of God (see Lk 3:38). Let's draw Adam. A stick figure will do:

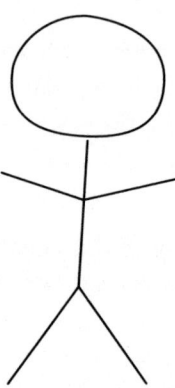

To indicate that he is God's son, I'm going to make him smiling and his face shining with God's glory:

What else does the Bible tell us about Adam? Genesis 2 tells us that God planted a garden in Eden and placed Adam there "to till it and keep it." There's a bit of a wordplay going on here. In the Hebrew language, this phrase is literally "to *serve*

The Covenant with Adam

(it) and to *guard* (it)." It is uncommon to find these two verbs together in the Bible. We will not find them together again until much later, in Numbers 3:7–8, where these two verbs—"serve" and "guard"—together describe what the priests do in the place of worship. For the ancient reader, Adam's commission to "serve and guard" in the garden would have had a priestly sound to it. Ancient readers probably understood Eden to be the original temple. Later temples were decorated to look like it.

This is the point: Adam had a priestly role in Eden, the original temple.

Let's put a stole on Adam to mark him off as a priest.

But that's not all! Adam had two other jobs besides his priesthood. In Genesis 1:26 and 28, Adam is given "dominion" over all other creatures on earth. I'll spare you all the language studies on the term "dominion" and cut to the chase: this is a kingly role. (You readers from Virginia, haven't you heard of King's Dominion amusement park?) Adam was king of all the living things on the earth. The ancient Jews took this for granted.

That's easy to illustrate. Let's put a crown on Adam.

Next, we see that, in Genesis 2:18–20, God gives Adam the job of naming the animals. That may not seem like a big deal to us, but in ancient times, giving a name was a very important privilege. Only the creator of something could grant a name to it—if you wrote a song, molded a sculpture, or produced a child, you had the right to name it—and no one else did. Here, God is making Adam his deputy and giving him a divine privilege—the right to name God's creatures. Not only that, but as Adam gives the creatures names, he is really speaking on behalf of God. What do we call a person who speaks on behalf of God? A prophet.

The Covenant with Adam 23

How shall we denote Adam as a prophet? The role of a prophet is to speak, so let's give him a big mouth:

There's one final role for Adam. The Bible tells us there was found no "helper fit for him" among the animals, so the LORD put him into a deep sleep and made the woman for him out of his rib. The next morning when Eve is brought to Adam, he bursts out in rather nice poetry:

> Bone of my bone
> and flesh of my flesh,
> she shall be called woman,
> because she was taken out of man.

Some consider this to be the first poetry found in the Bible. Through it, we see the civilizing effect that Eve has on Adam. Up to this point, he's just been sitting around naming animals: "Dog!" "Ape!" "Salamander!" Now he sees the woman, and he becomes The Bard, belting out sonnets in iambic pentameter (well, not quite, but you get the point). Perhaps the sacred author wants to point out that the arrival of woman is a high point in God's creation, and the woman brings out the best in the man.

In addition to being poetry, this elegant little statement of Adam's ("Bone of my bone," etc.) is covenant-making language. He is declaring her to be his kin (part of his family), and that's what you do in a covenant: make someone your kin. To this day, in most weddings, an unrelated man and woman go into a church (or courtroom), but when they come out they are Mr. and Mrs. John Q. Doe. Now they share a last name. They have become family. Here in Genesis we are witnessing the first groom and bride and the first "wedding," with God officiating. So we can fill in Adam's last role: bridegroom. For this, let's put a ring on his finger:

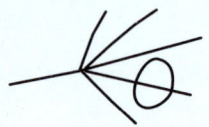

He's not just any bridegroom, either. He's the *universal* bridegroom. He's married to all humanity. Of course, "all humanity" at this point consists of only one other person. But still, he's married to the rest of the human race. This gives us our final portrait of Adam according to Genesis 1–2: firstborn son, king, priest, prophet, and bridegroom:

So What's the Point?

Why bother talking about Adam's roles? We began this chapter with the question "What is the meaning of life?" What is our purpose here on earth? The Bible addresses this question in the first chapters, by painting a picture of Adam that is a model for every human being. All of us are called to be sons (or daughters) of God, and therefore kings (queens), priests, prophets, and bridegrooms (brides).

What does that mean in practice? The *Catechism of the Catholic Church* discusses the roles of priest, prophet, and king in the lives of each Christian in paragraphs 901–913. But I'll make my own summary here:

Like Adam, we are to be kings. This does not mean, however, that we have to have political power and "rule" over other people. Jesus was not concerned with political power or very impressed with it. For example, Pontius Pilate, the Very Important Roman Governor of Judah, got frustrated with Jesus at one point and said, "Will you not speak to me? Don't you know I have the power to release you, and power to crucify you?" Jesus scarcely moved an eyebrow: "You would have no power over me unless it was given you from above" (Jn 19:11).

The kind of kingship that Jesus wants to give us is kingship over our selves, over sin, and over Satan. Anyone who doesn't master self, sin, and Satan is a slave, no matter how much political power he or she has. Jesus said, "Every one who commits sin is a slave to sin," yet, "If the Son makes you free, you will be free indeed" (Jn 8:34–36). What if Jesus had met Napoleon, or Stalin, or Mao face-to-face? Would he have been awed by them? Would he have considered them "kings" because of their military power? I don't think so. He would have seen these men as slaves of their own lusts, especially their lust for power. No one even starts to be a real king until he can rule himself. Jesus came to give us that power and authority to become kings over ourselves and then extend that reign over our homes, our jobs, and our families—whatever little piece of this world he gives into our hands.

A natural priesthood also flows from our status as children of God. A priest offers sacrifices to God. The sacrifice each one of us Christians offers is our own life. St. Paul wrote to the Christians in Rome, "I appeal to you . . . by the mercies of God, to present your bodies as a living sacrifice, holy and acceptable to God, which is your spiritual worship" (Rom 12:1). By "your bodies" St. Paul meant not just our physical bodies but our whole lives as well.

This priestly self-sacrifice of our lives is acted out in every Mass, when some laypeople bring forward the "gifts"—the bread and wine to be blessed by the priest and to become the Body and Blood of Jesus. I know we all tend to "check out" during this part of the Mass. Unless we know the people bringing forward the gifts, we start daydreaming about something else because it's not a part of the Mass where we have to stand, kneel, sing, or say anything. That's just human weakness, of course, but what is going on at that point in the Mass is in fact very important. The unblessed bread and wine represent the entire lives of all of us "laypeople," or better, us *common* priests. The *ministerial* priest then takes that bread and wine—our very lives—and calls down the Holy Spirit so that it becomes for us the Body and Blood of Jesus. Our lives are united to Christ, our many small sacrifices to his great Sacrifice.

That part of the Mass illustrates how the *ministerial* priesthood relates to the *common* priesthood of all believers. We need each other. We need our parish priests to give us the divine power of the sacraments so that we have the strength to fulfill our priestly duty to offer our entire lives as a sacrifice to God for the salvation of the world. Yet our priests need us, too. Just as the Mass could not be celebrated if there was no bread and wine brought forward, our ministerial priests could not fulfill their calling without us common priests. Without us they would, in a sense, have nothing to do. We are the "raw material" they need to bless and transform into the Body of Christ, the Church.

In addition to being priests, God calls us (through baptism) to be prophets, that is, to speak God's word to the world. Does that mean we have to preach or predict the future? Not necessarily. Although the prophets did predict future events, their first job was to share God's word and explain to the people what God wanted them to do. Every time we share some of God's truth with our children, spouse, friend, co-worker, or a stranger on the bus, we are fulfilling our prophetic calling.

Finally, like Adam, we are intended for relationship with another person, or perhaps better, for another Person. That's the meaning for us of Adam's status as "universal bridegroom." It's not that each one of us is called to marriage in this life (although many of us are), much less that each of us is intended to be married to everyone else! Only Jesus can fill Adam's shoes as Bridegroom for humanity. But each one of us is called to "nuptiality," a term theologians use to describe the real meaning behind weddings and marriage. Each one of us is intended for a relationship with another Person (theologians call this "communion"), a relationship so intimate that the Bible frequently describes it with the language of marriage. That relationship is with Jesus Christ.

A holy marriage between Christian spouses is a wonderful thing, and it gives us a glimpse of what awaits us in heaven. Yet still it is only a glimpse. Our relationship with Christ in heaven will be much more blessed than even the best marriage on earth. St. Paul says, "No eye has seen, nor ear heard, nor the heart of man conceived, what God has prepared for those who love him" (1 Cor 2:9). Not only that, but this relationship begins *now*. If we let go of our sins, we begin to taste the sweetness of that communion with Jesus already in this life.

Son of God, king, priest, prophet, and bridegroom—these are the roles Adam enjoyed in his covenant with God at the beginning of human history, before sin messed everything up. These are also the roles we're called to. They are the meaning of our life. We don't live up to them perfectly. Only Jesus did and does; that's why St. Paul calls Jesus the "last Adam" and the "Second Man" (1 Cor 15:45–49).

Putting the Finishing Touches on Eden

We've learned a lot in this chapter about the purpose of creation and the purpose of man. Now it is time to draw a little sketch that summarizes some key features of the Adamic or Creation Covenant.

A central feature is Mount Eden, which is fairly simple to draw:

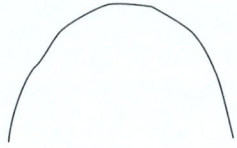

We know Eden was a mountain because rivers flowed out of it to water the whole earth (Gn 2:10–14). Since water flows from high ground to low, Eden must have been the highest point on the earth. That was, in fact, the general belief of the Israelites as well as the other peoples of the ancient Near East. The prophet Ezekiel confirms this when he calls Eden "the holy mountain of God" (Ez 28:14). Here, we will stay simple by drawing one large river flowing from Eden:

The idea of a river flowing from the mountain of God will be very important in other parts of scripture, farther down the road.

Besides the river, we can add a few more features to our picture of Eden. Genesis 2:11–12 lets us know that gold and precious stones were available near Eden. That is important, because most temples in the ancient world were decorated with gold and precious stones. We modern readers don't usually understand this, but ancient readers knew that Eden was the model for temple building. Many temples throughout the ancient world were built and decorated to look like the original divine garden.

So let's add some gold and precious stones to our sketch:

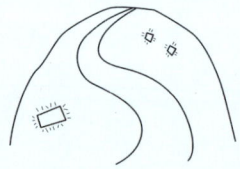

Another prominent feature of Eden was the presence of wonderful fruit trees, especially the Tree of Life and the Tree of the Knowledge of Good and Evil. Let's at least add the Tree of Life to our sketch:

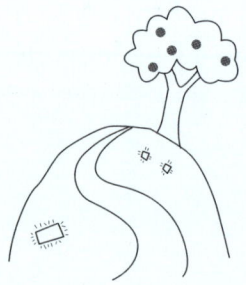

We know from other parts of scripture (Ez 28:14) that angels (called "cherubim") were present in Eden, even though

The Covenant with Adam

they only get mentioned near the end of the story (Gn 3:24). An angel, plus Adam and Eve, complete our sketch:

This is where we are in salvation history so far. Adam and Eve are dwelling at peace with God in Eden, the garden-mountain that was the original "sanctuary," the model for all future temples. King and queen of all creation, they enjoy harmony with the animals, plants, and all created things. All their natural needs are met by the garden God planted for them. Their supernatural needs were met by God himself, who (it seems) would come to "walk" with them in the garden (Gn 3:8).

Self-Study Guide

Background

What is the purpose for which God made the world? This is the essential question of the Genesis creation accounts. In seven days God essentially built a temple-universe or a building of creation. The connection between creation and a temple is verified in other scripture passages and other ancient writings from the same time as Genesis. The creation accounts also take on the creation of Adam, the first man, and answer the question about the purpose of his life. In fact, like some of his descendants, Adam was a king, priest, and prophet. When he effectively married Eve, he was also a bridegroom. All of these roles of Adam help us to find meaning and purpose in our own life.

Reading Comprehension

1. What does the first verse in Genesis 1 state?
2. What is the meaning of the Hebrew phrase *tohu wabohu*?
3. What did God create on the third day of creation? Repeat the drawing to represent the creation on the third day.
4. What is one reason that the building of creation can be depicted as a temple?
5. What is the fancy theological term for being a son (or daughter) of God and made in his own likeness and image?

The Covenant with Adam

6. What does it mean to say that Adam is the "universal bridegroom"?
7. Why does St. Paul call Jesus the "last Adam" or "Second Man"?

Reading in Context

In your notebook, answer the following questions, referencing outside sources as needed.

1. Explain the argument between "Creationism" and "Darwinism."
2. Define "cosmos" as relates to the creation of the world.
3. What is a "stole"? What does it represent in regard to priesthood?
4. Use the word "dominion" in a sentence.
5. Explain the difference between the *common* priesthood and the *ministerial* priesthood.
6. What does it mean to say that Eden was a "sanctuary"?

Writing Assignment

Answer the following questions in two to three well-constructed paragraphs.

- What is the meaning of life?
- How does the life of Adam help you to answer that question?

Small-Group Guide

Opening Prayer

Loving Father,

Thank you for this precious gift of your Word, through which we may come to know and worship you more fully and love you more deeply.

Lord Jesus Christ, today we gather as your disciples. We sit at your feet ready to listen to your Word. We humbly ask that you open our ears so that we may hear with our intellect and open our hearts so that we may know you intimately.

Come, Holy Spirit; fill us with your gifts of wisdom, understanding, and knowledge so that we may grow in love, faithfulness, and joy. Amen.

Discussion Questions

1. By establishing the setting of humanity's story in God's creation, Eden is described as the first "sanctuary" (page 31).

   Define sanctuary. It has both secular and religious connotations. List both.

2. God then created Adam and placed him in this sanctuary, Eden.

   Describe yourself as a creation of God. We are made in his "likeness and image." What does this mean to you?

Identify those qualities that make you uniquely you. Describe yourself as a child of God. Include vocabulary specific to family relationships.

3. God created the earth (and the universe!) as a temple and placed Adam at the center of this place of worship.

    Like Adam, we find ourselves in the dual role of children of God and stewards of this beautiful temple. How does this knowledge of your identity change, augment, or otherwise inform the ways in which you see yourself?

4. Examine your life through the lens of the Adamic Covenant discussed in this chapter. We are baptized as priest, prophet, and king. We are also sons and daughters of the Father, and, finally, we are "bridegrooms" because we are called to relationship with the Lord.

    How does recognizing ourselves in these roles empower and enrich how we live our faith?

5. What tangible steps can you take to grow in faith?

    Select one of the roles discussed in this chapter: priest, prophet, king, child of God, or bridegroom. Create a plan to develop this area of your faith life. The plan can include prayer, spiritual reading, developing a habit, or seeking spiritual direction, to name a few possibilities. The options are as unique as you.

Bonus: In your notebook, draw a stick figure of yourself, joyful in your role as child of God. Add a symbol of your desire to grow in faith.

Closing Prayer

Heavenly Father,

Thank you for your Fatherhood. We are grateful for the lives you have given us and for the world in which we live.

We praise you and glorify you in word and deed as we strive to fulfill our roles in your Creation. Bless us in our endeavor to live fully your teachings. Amen.

TWO
WASHING UP AND STARTING OVER
The Covenant with Noah

Suggested Reading: Genesis 3-9

The Sad Story from Adam to Noah

At the end of Genesis 2, we are at a highpoint: the newly married Mr. and Mrs. Adam are living in their palatial garden paradise and enjoying a close relationship with their Father-God.

But we all know the good times didn't last for long. At the beginning of Genesis 3, a snake shows up. Snakes are almost never a good thing in the Old Testament.

In the present case, the snake begins to cast doubt on the trustworthiness of God and his word. God had told Adam and Eve not to eat from the Tree of the Knowledge of Good and Evil because it would lead to their death. But the snake presses Eve on the point. "Did God *really* say . . . ?" the snake begins and goes on to outright contradict what God had told Adam and

Eve: "You will *not* die. . . . For God knows when you eat of it . . . you will be like God" (Gn 3:1–4; emphasis mine).

The snake's basic message is this: "You can't trust God as your loving Father. His rules aren't for your good. He just doesn't want you to experience the kind of life he enjoys."

Eve buys this line. Looking at the apple, she sees it is tasty, pretty, and will make her smart as God—so why not eat it? She also gives some to Adam, and he eats (Gn 3:6).

Adam has been strangely passive in this whole affair, although he seems to be nearby. What's been going on? Why doesn't he say or do anything? We want to ask: "Hey, Adam, what about your duty to 'guard' the garden? How did this snake get in here?"

The snake promised them godlike knowledge when they ate of the fruit. Instead, the only real knowledge they gain from eating the fruit is to find out . . . they're naked! They also experience new sensations: shame and fear. When God comes in the afternoon, they can't go out to walk and talk with him as usual. They hide—as if it were possible to escape the Father who made them.

When God finally tracks them down, Adam accepts no responsibility for eating the fruit: "The Woman whom you gave to me, she gave me the fruit, and I ate" (Gn 3:12). Notice this clever ploy, which middle managers and bureaucrats have been using ever since: pass the buck both up and down the chain of command at the same time. "The *woman*"—it's all her fault—"whom *you* gave me"—and it's your fault, too, God, for giving her to me! Eve can't (or won't) top Adam's evasion of responsibility: "The snake tricked me, and I ate" (Gn 3:13).

In the following verses, God administers a punishment appropriate to each of the three guilty parties, and Adam and Eve are removed from the Garden where they had access to the tree of life (Gn 3:14–23).

God places a cherub (a guardian angel) on the east side of Eden, to keep Adam away (Gn 3:24). Why doesn't he just walk around to the north, west, or south? As mentioned above, the ancient readers would have known that Eden was not just a garden but also a temple, and the ancient Israelite temple had only one entrance, facing east.

So is God a petty tyrant, throwing Adam and Eve out because they broke his little rule? No. A son who distrusts his Father and joins up with his Father's enemies can't stay living in the family home. A priest who doesn't have faith in the words of his God can't stay serving in the temple. God doesn't have many options in this matter, especially since there seems to be little in the way of repentance or apologies coming from any of the guilty parties.

He does kindly clothe Adam and Eve in skins, which made much better clothing than fig leaves they had been using. (Leather is still used for clothing, but leaf garments, for some odd reason, have never really caught on.) Of course, skins have to come from somewhere. You can't get skins without killing an animal, which points out an interesting aspect of the story. God told Adam and Eve that they would die when they ate the fruit. But they don't die. Something else dies in their place, and they are clothed in the skin of the dead animal. We don't know what animal (or animals) died and gave its skin to Adam and Eve, but it's often thought to be a lamb, based on biblical imagery.

There is a foreshadowing going on here. When he clothes Adam and Eve in the skin of the dead lamb, God is pointing forward to what will have to happen for Adam and Eve's disobedience to be completely fixed. A different Lamb of God is going to have to die to take away the sins of the world and clothe humans in his righteousness (see Is 53:7 and 61:10).

Although he clothes Adam and Eve with animal skins, God does not want them to eat from the fruit of the tree of life—not out of a desire to punish them but because he doesn't want Adam and Eve to become immortal—and forever stuck—in their disobedient, rebellious condition.

In many ways, the rest of the story of the Bible, and the rest of the history of humankind, will be one, long road back to the Tree of Life, to Eden, and to divine childhood.

East of Eden

Things don't get better when Adam and Eve are out on their own. Their oldest son, Cain, murders the younger Abel and then begins to populate the earth with his descendants, some of whom are more wicked than he was and even begin to do wrong-headed things like take two wives (Gn 4:19). This goes from bad to worse, until the "Sons of God" start taking as many wives as they want from the "Daughters of Men" in Genesis 6:1–5. People have puzzled over who is meant by the "Sons of God" since ancient times. The ancients often thought they were fallen angels. St. Augustine said they were the righteous descendants of Seth, Adam's third son. Some modern scholars suggest they were royalty, since "Son of God" was a term used for kings in antiquity. We can rule out fallen angels, but the other two interpretations are possibilities.

The multiple marriages (polygamy) of the "Sons of God" result in children who become "men of renown," or better, "men of notoriety" (Gn 6:4). These "notorious" descendants of these polygamous relationships seem to offend God, and the reason may have a commonsense explanation. Polygamous fathers have too many sons to properly parent. Wild, fatherless sons grow up to be a danger to other people and lead a society into chaos. Such chaos is described in Genesis 6:5: "The LORD saw that the wickedness of man was great in the earth, and that every imagination of the thoughts of his heart was only evil continually."

God's response is to back up and start over. The evil actions of these "notorious" descendants provoke God to clean the earth with a flood and begin again, almost from scratch. God allows the world to return to a state of "tohu wabohu," with his Spirit (often translated "wind") moving over the face of the waters once more (compare Gn 1:2 with Gn 8:1). Then, for a second time, he pulls the dry land out of the water in an act of re-creation.

The Rising of a New Son: Noah and His Covenant

Noah and his family mark a new beginning for the human race. One may wonder, why just Noah? Why didn't God save the rest of humanity from the flood? The New Testament reveals that Noah was the only one interested in being saved (Heb 11:7). Noah is remembered as a "preacher of righteousness" who rebuked his contemporaries for what they were doing while he was building the ark (2 Pt 2:5). But no one paid any attention to the crazy man building the big boat, even though he was preaching and building a long time.

As I remarked above, the flood plunged the earth into a watery chaos that resembled the situation of "tohu wabohu" before God began the six days of creation. When the dry land reemerges 150 days later, Noah and his buoyant "zoological garden" (a "floating Eden") land on the top of Mount Ararat, a new mountain of God.

We can begin to sketch this out. First, Mount Ararat:

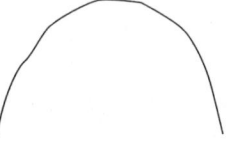

Now we can make the ark, which was a boxy, barge-like structure:

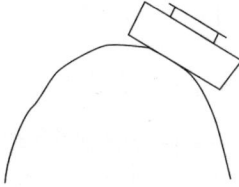

If we want to get fancy, we can open the door of the ark and let the giraffes and snakes out:

The Covenant with Noah

When Noah emerges from the ark, he performs a priestly act: he builds an altar and offers a sacrifice to God.

The Bible speaks of God "smelling the aroma" of the sacrifice and being moved with compassion for humanity and all creation. He makes a covenant with Noah:

> Then God said to Noah and to his sons with him, "Behold, I establish my covenant with you and your descendants after you, and with every living creature that is with you. . . . And God said, "This is the sign of the covenant which I make between me and you and every living creature that is with you, for all future generations: I set my bow in the cloud . . . God said to Noah, "This is the sign of the covenant which I have established between me and all flesh that is upon the earth." (Gn 9:8–13)

God seals his covenant with Noah using a "sign," in this case, a rainbow:

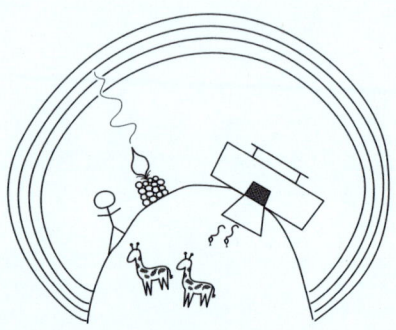

What is the significance of this covenant? Earlier in Genesis 9, God spoke to Noah and his sons using words we have heard before:

> And God blessed Noah and his sons, and said to them, "Be fruitful and multiply, and fill the earth. The fear of you and the dread of you shall be upon every beast of the earth, and upon every bird of the air, upon everything that creeps on the ground and all the fish of the sea; into your hand they are delivered. Every moving thing that lives shall be food for you; and as I gave you the green plants, I give you everything. . . . And you, be fruitful and multiply, bring forth abundantly on the earth and multiply in it." (Gn 9:1–7)

All this language recalls Genesis 1 and God's original covenant relationship with Adam. So we can say that this covenant with Noah is, in a sense, a renewal of the covenant with Adam. Only things are not quite as good any more: for example, now there is fear between man and the animals.

Despite the imperfections, the covenant with Noah brings us hope. Although the world is not perfect, humanity (Noah

The Covenant with Noah

and his family) is back in a relationship with God. The flood is a re-creation, and Noah, the new Adam.

This is how far we have progressed in salvation history:

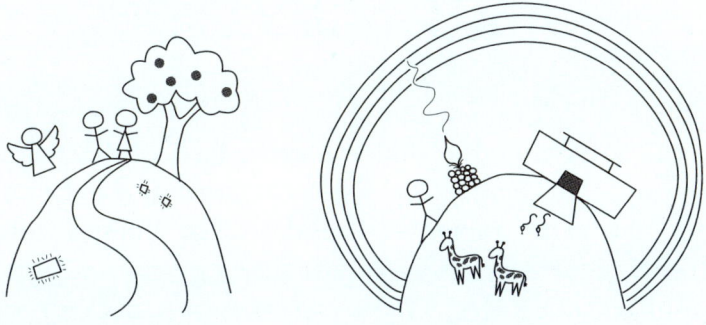

Adamic Covenant   Noahic Covenant

Self-Study Guide

Background

God's covenant with Noah is part of the next stage of his revelation. The covenant revealed the precepts of the Law and combatted paganism, a combination of idolatry (idol worship), polytheism (worship of many gods), and polygamy (multiple marriages). God's response was to back up and start over. The language of God's covenant with Noah resembles the language of the first covenant with Adam. The covenant with Noah is a "second creation story."

Reading Comprehension

1. What is the snake's basic message to Adam and Eve?
2. Why is God's punishment of Adam and Eve—removing them from the Garden of Eden—an appropriate punishment?
3. What is foreshadowed in God's clothing of Adam and Eve in the skins of dead lambs?
4. What are two possible interpretations for the term "sons of God" in Genesis 6:1–5?
5. Where does the chaos described in Genesis 6:5 arise?
6. What is God's response to the "notorious" descendants of Adam and Eve?
7. Why did God only save Noah and not the rest of humanity?

The Covenant with Noah

8. What does Noah do when he emerges from the ark?
9. How does God seal the covenant with Noah?
10. What is the significance of the covenant with Noah?

Reading in Context

In your notebook, write a one-word answer for each clue. The box below the clues contains letter groupings for the one-word answers; two or more letter groupings are needed for each answer. The letter groupings appear just once. The numbers in parenthesis after the clues indicate the number of letters in each answer. All of the answers appear in this chapter.

1. A guardian angel (6)
2. Adam's third son (4)
3. Multiple marriages (8)
4. Accepting what others do without an active response (7)
5. Well known for a bad quality (9)
6. A cruel, oppressive ruler (6)

TH	PO	LYG	RUB
NOT	TY	OUS	VE
NT	AMY	ORI	SE
CHE	PA	SSI	RA

Answers: (1) cherub; (2) Seth; (3) polygamy; (4) passive; (5) notorious; (6) tyrant

Writing Assignment

Read from the *Catechism of the Catholic Church*, 2415–2418, on respect for the integrity of creation. Then write two to three paragraphs on what implications the Noah story has on today's environmental issues.

Small-Group Guide

Opening Prayer

Loving Father,

Thank you for this precious gift of your Word, through which we may come to know and worship you more fully and love you more deeply.

Lord Jesus Christ, today we gather as your disciples. We sit at your feet ready to listen to your Word. We humbly ask that you open our ears so that we may hear with our intellect and open our hearts so that we may know you intimately.

Come, Holy Spirit; fill us with your gifts of wisdom, understanding, and knowledge so that we may grow in love, faithfulness, and joy. Amen.

Discussion Questions

1. Adam and Eve broke the covenant with God, and that act of disobedience carried consequences for them and for us. What are these consequences? List the punishments described as they pertain to Adam and Eve. Explain how Adam and Eve's sin has consequences for us.

   God is compassionate and merciful—a God of second chances (and more!). Describe God's mercy in Adam's and Eve's lives. Describe how he extended his mercy to all humanity by creating a covenant with Noah.

2. How do we use our knowledge of God's mercy in our day-to-day living? We see a broken covenant made anew in Noah. In fact, as we continue

reading, we'll see how God renews these covenants time and again.

Think of a part of your life that needs renewal, mercy, or forgiveness. Implement a plan to address this through intentional action, whether that is prayer, reaching out to someone, or making a change in behavior. It can be as simple as receiving the Sacrament of Reconciliation.

3. God's mercy is evident in his desire to bring us back to him each time we fail. He loves us! Share a time in your life when you felt weighed down by doubt or despair. Where did you find the hope and fortitude to recover? What can you learn from this experience to help carry you forward the next time you encounter a spiritual doubt?

4. God's plan for us is perfect. We are not. Yet our loving Father is moved with compassion for us and offers us his love and forgiveness at each misstep we make.

    Consider an action or a small step that you can take to renew your commitment to God. What can you do today to start anew?

Bonus: In your notebook, draw a stick figure of yourself, joyful in your role as child of God. Add a symbol of hope.

Closing Prayer

Compassionate Father,

Thank you for your mercy. We are grateful for the waves of your compassion that wash over us, cleanse us, and make us new in the Spirit.

We praise you and glorify you in word and deed as we strive to live in perfect relationship with you. Bless us in our endeavor to live fully your teachings. Amen.

THREE
A NEW HOPE
The Covenant with Abraham

Suggested Reading: Genesis 10-17, 20-22

The Sad Story from Noah to Abraham

We ended the last chapter on a high note, with Noah, the New Adam, disembarking and beginning a new chapter in the history of humankind. Unfortunately, this new chapter quickly begins to sound a lot like the old chapter.

Already in Genesis 9, we read about a certain "fall" of Noah that bears a striking resemblance to an earlier "fall." Noah drinks wine, the fruit of his vineyard, and gets drunk and naked in his tent. His son Ham goes into the tent, "sees his father's nakedness," and makes fun of him to his brothers. Shem and Japheth walk in backward and cover their father's "nakedness." When Noah awakes, he realizes he has been violated and curses Ham's son Canaan.

This story is very strange to us and raises many questions. Why was Ham's sin so serious? Why did Noah feel violated? Why curse Canaan rather than Ham himself? There are possible answers to all these questions, but all of them involve complicated studies of the original language of this story, which would bog us down. For now, let's just make a few points. First, the Hebrew phrase "see his father's nakedness" suggests a much more serious offense than simply seeing Noah in his birthday suit. Second, the themes of this story are ones we have seen somewhere before: (1) the consumption of fruit (here grapes, as wine), (2) nakedness, (3) shame, and (4) curse. These, of course, are the themes of Adam and Eve's fall in the Garden of Eden. The story of Noah's nakedness is really the story of the fall of the New Adam. Noah gives in to foolish indulgence. This starts a chain of events bringing disharmony and sin back into the human family. It becomes clear that the flood has not solved the problems of humanity. All the "bad people" have been washed away. "Good people" were saved in the ark. But the problem is that the line between good and bad does not run cleanly between groups of people; it runs down the center of each person. Sin has infected every human being. St. Paul puts it like this: "All have sinned and fallen short of the glory of God" (Rom 3:23)—even Noah.

If things went downhill quickly after the Fall in Eden, they do so again after Noah's fall. It only took two chapters to get from Eden to the worldwide rebellion of the "Sons of God" and their polygamous ways (Gn 6). Now it takes only one chapter to get from Noah's drunkenness to the Tower of Babel (Gn 11). The Babel story is kind of a parallel to the Sons of God–Daughters of Men account. In each case, we have a widespread rebellion of humanity against God, followed by God's response: first the flood, then the confusion of languages.

In the aftermath of Babel, humanity is scattered across the earth in disharmony. The family relationship with God has been broken. How can this situation ever be fixed?

The Covenant with Abraham

At this point, God makes a decisive choice that will permanently alter the flow of the river of history. He chooses one man, a certain "Chaldean" (a person from a land that is part of present-day Iraq) named Abram. God chooses this man to bring back blessing to the rest of the human family.

We read of this in Genesis 12:1–3:

> Now the LORD said to Abram, "Go from your country and your kindred and your father's house to the land that I will show you. And I will make of you a great nation, and I will bless you, and make your name great, so that you will be a blessing. I will bless those who bless you, and him who curses you I will curse; and in you all the families of the earth shall be blessed."

Notice that Abraham is not chosen for his own sake. He is chosen so that he can bless the rest of the human family. Verse 2 ends by saying, "You will be a blessing," and verse 3 ends with the promise "in you all the families of the earth shall be blessed." By "all the families of the earth," the Bible is referring to Genesis 10, which is a list of the seventy ethnic groups that make up humanity, from the ancient Israelite perspective. It is important to realize that the Old Testament is a book about salvation and blessing for all human beings. Many people think the Old Testament is a Jewish book about salvation for the Jews alone. But the whole reason the Jews are special is because their ancestor Abram was chosen by God *to bring blessing to everyone*. This has always been God's mission for Abram's descendants.

The Bible lists all the nations of the earth in Genesis 10, describes how they lost God's favor in Genesis 11, and shows how they will get God's blessing back in Genesis 12: "In you, Abram, all the families of the earth will be blessed."

Three Blessings to Abram

The Bible introduces Abram out of the blue, without giving much of his back story. All we know is that he's a descendant of Shem, and he's living in modern-day Iraq with his family. Then, suddenly, God appears to him and speaks to him. Probably the story about who Abram was and why God seems to know and like him so much was too long for the biblical author to tell. We'll just have to trust him on that.

Let's look more closely at God's first words to Abram in Genesis 12:1–3:

> Now the LORD said to Abram, "Go from your country and your kindred and your father's house to the land that I will show you. And I will make of you a great nation, and I will bless you, and make your name great, so that you will be a blessing. I will bless those who bless you, and him who curses you I will curse; and in you all the families of the earth shall be blessed."

In among these general blessings, there are three specific things God promises to Abram: (1) a great nation, (2) a great name, and (3) a blessing to everyone.

God gives these three promises to Abram in chapter 12 as *simple promises,* but later in the story of Abram, God is going to affirm each promise in a more serious way. He is going to work each promise into a formal *covenant.* The difference between a promise and a covenant is like the difference between an engagement ring and a wedding ring. One symbolizes a strong hope, a firm intention; the other symbolizes an unbreakable commitment.

The Covenant with Abraham

The first time God takes one of these promises and makes it into a covenant is several chapters later, in Genesis 15. The situation is this: God comes to speak to Abram, and encourages him, but Abram is upset because he doesn't have any children, even though God promised them. God tells him not to worry about it; it will happen in time. But Abram wants more reassurance. So God tells him to bring a bunch of animals, lay them out, and cut them in half:

Then everything gets dark, and a torch and firepot appear and proceed to move between the animal pieces as God speaks to Abram:

Now, if you're like me, this whole scene seems very weird. It reminds me of the ceremony Huckleberry Finn believed would cure warts: swinging a dead cat over your head in a graveyard at midnight. What are strange ceremonies like this doing in the Bible?

The Covenant with Abraham

Actually, ancient readers would immediately have recognized the ritual God and Abram perform in Genesis 15 as a typical *covenant-making* ceremony. The Jewish tradition calls this event "the covenant between the pieces."

Like all ceremonies, the actions had meaning. When people would cut up animals and walk between them, it meant "if I do not keep my covenant commitments, may I be killed like these animals." It was like calling down a curse of death on yourself if you didn't do what was promised, like the childhood oath: "Cross my heart and hope to die, stick a needle in my eye . . ."

The torch and firepot represented God's presence. Fire is a sign of God's presence in many places in the Bible: think of the pillar of fire that will later lead the Israelites in the desert after they escape from Egypt, or the tongues of fire that came to rest on the Apostles at Pentecost. When the burning torch and firepot moved through the pieces of the animals, God was saying, "If I don't keep my word to you, Abram, may I be cut to pieces just like these animals."

You may ask, "How can God call down a curse on himself?" It seems in credible, but God was coming down to Abram's human level and taking part in a ceremony Abram would understand. Coming down to a human level is what scholars call *divine condescension (CON-de-SEN-shun)*.

So God is making a covenant with Abram here, and the covenant makes them family. Most covenants also had special rules, promises, or instructions attached, which would show how the new family should run. Genesis 15 fits this pattern. God gives some special promises as part of this covenant, in verses 4–5, 15–16, and 18–21. Taken together, these verses promise at least two important things: Abram will have lots of descendants (v. 5) who will possess lots of land (vv. 18–21). Lots of people and lots of land are the two ingredients you need for a great nation. So we can say, the first promise to Abram (great nationhood) has been worked into (or "incorporated into") a covenant with God.

The Fall of Abram

What have we seen so far immediately after every biblical covenant is made? A fall, right? So it is here. No sooner does God make a covenant with Abram in Genesis 15 than we get a kind of "mini-fall" of Abram in Genesis 16. In this chapter, Abram and Sarah begin to doubt if God's plan to give them children is going to work out the normal way, so they decide to help God out a little bit with the assistance of some ancient "reproductive technology." Abram listens to his wife's bad idea (a parallel with the Fall in Eden) and takes Sarah's maid Hagar as a second wife and surrogate mother. According to legal custom in those days, the maid Hagar's children would belong to her mistress Sarah. The plan "works," in the sense that a son, Ishmael, is born, but this son is not the person God was intending as Abram's heir, and the whole episode just causes fighting, arguing, envy, and unhappiness in Abram's family. (Almost every time someone takes more than one wife in the Bible, it leads to trouble. The Bible is trying to teach a lesson: stick with monogamy. I call this biblical theme "the implicit critique of polygamy.")

The Covenant Renewed

The birth of this unintended heir, Ishmael, forces God to intervene and "clean things up" in the next chapter. Genesis 17 begins with the Lord saying to Abram, "I am God Almighty: walk before me and be blameless" (v. 1). There's a bit of a rebuke intended here. It's like God is saying, "Pay attention to me, and clean up your act."

The Covenant with Abraham

In the next verses, God repeats the promise of great nationhood from Genesis 15 and adds to it. He also promises, for the first time, that kings will come from Abram, and that Abram will be the father of many nations. Actually, these two promises are related to each other and to the promise of a "great name" from Genesis 12:2.

In ancient times, the term "great name" was connected to kings. Ancient kings were the ones thought to have great names. Furthermore, kings were known as "fathers" of their countries. Emperors, who ruled over not just one but many nationalities and ethnic groups, were "fathers of many nations." Therefore, the promises that Abram would be the ancestor of kings and would become the "father of a multitude of nations" both point to the same reality: Abram's descendants would include great kings with great names, who would in fact become emperors and "fathers of many nations." So the promises to Abram would be fulfilled in his descendants.

As if to highlight the connection with the promise of a great name, God actually gives Abram a greater name: he lengthens it to *Abraham* (v. 5). God also gives Abraham a covenant duty to perform, which will mark himself and his descendants as God's family. This covenant duty is circumcision. The ceremony of circumcision presents obvious difficulties for illustration, so I'm just going to draw a big knife. We'll know what it means:

People have wondered about the meaning of circumcision. Why make Abraham go through with this procedure? One possibility is that circumcision is connected with how Abraham went astray in Genesis 16, by sleeping with Hagar. Circumcision might be a symbolic rebuke of the part of the body Abraham used when he messed up God's plan in chapter 16.

Another possibility—which doesn't rule out the one just mentioned—is that when Abraham cut off that piece of skin, it was as much as saying, "If I don't keep my covenant duties to God, may I be 'cut off' (killed) like this piece of flesh!"

In Genesis 15, Abraham cut animals, but in Genesis 17, he has to cut *himself*. We are definitely raising the bar and upping the ante here. The things Abraham has to do for the covenant are becoming more serious.

Speaking of cutting, it's interesting to note that, in Hebrew, you don't "make" a covenant; you actually "cut" a covenant. This was because covenant-making ceremonies usually involved cutting something. Cutting produced blood, and the blood had a double meaning: on the one hand, the two covenant parties now shared one blood—they were family. On the other hand, if one of the covenant parties broke the covenant—"then let his blood be shed, just like this blood we are shedding now!"

God's final act in Genesis 17 is to clear up who will be the covenant heir. Ishmael was born in Genesis 16, but not of Sarah, Abraham's first (and should have been "only") wife. God makes it plain: Ishmael will receive a blessing and will become a great nation himself, but the covenant is going to pass to Sarah's son Isaac.

The next chapters explain how things worked out. Isaac was indeed born in time (Gn 21), and Hagar and Ishmael were disinherited but taken care of by God (Gn 21:8–21). Once

Abraham makes peace with the natives in the land (Gn 21:22–34), it seems that now, at last, Abraham and Sarah will live happily ever after.

But not before Abraham gets the biggest test of his life.

The Final Covenant with Abraham

By the end of Genesis 21, nearly everything seems to have worked out for Abraham. Still, there is a nagging sense that something has not yet been done. The promises of great nation and great name have been worked into the covenant between God and Abraham, but the last and best promise, of universal blessing to the whole human family, has not been mentioned since Genesis 12:3. What's going to happen to that promise? Is it ever going to become part of the covenant?

The answer comes in Genesis 22. But first, God wants to see if Abraham—and Isaac, too—are the right kinds of persons to bring blessing to the rest of humanity.

So the chapter begins, "After these things, God tested Abraham" (Gn 22:1).

He calls to Abraham, and in words that sound like God's first call to Abram in Genesis 12:1, he tells him to take his son Isaac and "go to the land of Moriah, to a mountain that I will show you." There, Abraham is to take his "only son" (or "only begotten son") Isaac and offer him as a sacrifice.

Abraham does as the Lord commands. He and his son travel to the mountain God shows him. Once there, he lays Isaac on the altar and gets ready to kill him.

Of course, the obvious question is, how can God command Abraham to kill his own son? Isn't that barbaric? It conjures up images of old man Abraham overpowering little five-year-old Isaac and tossing him cruelly on the logs before dispatching him with a knife. Biblical child abuse of the worst kind! Or is it?

The only answer for this question is to read the text more carefully. One of the first things to note is: who carries the wood up the mountain for the sacrifice? When we look carefully, we see it's *Isaac,* not *Abraham.* Clearly, then, Isaac is the stronger of the two, because the wood needed for a sacrifice was a very heavy load. Abraham only carries the fire and the knife. So we should not see an old man and a child; we should see an old man and a strapping teenager. Therefore, when Abraham later binds Isaac and places him on the altar, we can be sure that Isaac has fully cooperated. There was no way Abraham could have controlled his younger, stronger son. No, for Isaac, this was "a death he freely accepted." He "entered willingly" into his sacrifice.

Several features of this story should give us what I call "pre-jà vu." When something happens to us that feels strikingly familiar or reminds us of something else that happened to us in the past, we say "déjà vu" ("already seen" in French). But when we see something strikingly familiar in the Old Testament that reminds us of something we know about, but hasn't happened yet in biblical history, I like to say "pre-jà vu."

Where else in the Bible do we see a "one and only" or "only begotten" son carrying the wood of his own sacrifice up a hill, there to be sacrificed by his father to God? Calvary, of course! So the sacrifice of Isaac on the mountain in Genesis 22 is a premonition of Christ's sacrifice on the cross. I tell my students, "Genesis 22 is the Calvary of the Old Testament."

St. John actually makes the connection between Isaac and Jesus in what is probably the most famous verse of the Bible, John 3:16: "For God so loved the world that he gave his *only begotten* Son, that whoever believes in him will not perish but have everlasting life."

The phrase "only begotten" is one word in Greek, *monogenes.* It is a very rare Greek word, and it is probably a literal translation of the Hebrew word *yahid,* which means "one and only." *Yahid* is also a very rare word, yet it is used three times in Genesis 22 to describe Isaac: in verses 2, 12, and 16. My favorite Bible version (the RSV Second Catholic Edition) translates every occurrence as "only begotten," in order to pick up the connection with John 3:16. It's a good translation because St. John *does* want to show us that Jesus is a New Isaac. In fact, he is much greater than Isaac because he goes through with the sacrifice and actually dies. Jesus dies on the cross because he is, as the Mass says, "The Lamb of God who takes away the sins of the world."

Abraham hints at the coming of Jesus as the Lamb of God already in Genesis 22. As Abraham and Isaac are walking up the mountain, Isaac asks his father, "Behold, the fire and the wood; but where is the lamb for a burnt offering?" Abraham replies, "*God will provide himself the lamb for a burnt offering, my son*" (Gn 22:8).

The natural sense of Abraham's statement is that "God will provide *for himself* a lamb for the sacrifice." The day will come, however, when Abraham's words will take on a deeper sense, a day when God will, in fact, provide *himself* as the lamb for the burnt offering.

The natural meaning of Abraham's prophecy is fulfilled right there in Genesis 22, when the angel of God will stop Abraham from sacrificing Isaac and substitute a ram caught in nearby bushes. The deeper sense will be fulfilled almost at this same spot some two thousand years later, when Abraham's descendant, Jesus of Nazareth, will be laid on the wood and slain, the true "Lamb of God who takes away the sins of the world" (Jn 1:29).

We can see, then, why the Bible calls Abraham a "prophet" (Gn 20:7). In a sense, he is the first person in scripture to predict Jesus's sacrifice on the cross. His son Isaac acts out the role Jesus will play in the drama at Calvary so many years in the future.

The connection between Isaac and Jesus is all the more striking because of the location. Abraham is told to sacrifice Isaac on a mountain in the land of Moria (Gn 22:2). This mountain was later called "Mount Moriah," and it is the location that King Solomon chose to build the temple (2 Chr 3:1), which was within sight of Calvary, the nearby hill where Jesus made his self-sacrifice.

In light of the whole Bible, the story of Abraham and Isaac in Genesis 22 is not about ancient practices of human sacrifice or bizarre cases of child abuse. In Genesis 22, God invited Abraham and Isaac to take part in the very kind of sacrifice that God the Holy Trinity would have to undergo so many years later in order to save humanity from sin and death. God was as much as saying to Abraham and Isaac, "Are you willing to undergo the kind of sacrifice I will have to undergo in order to restore blessing to all humanity?"

"Are you, Father Abraham, willing to part with your only begotten Son?"

"Are you, Son Isaac, willing to die in obedience to your Father, out of love for God?"

Isaac and Abraham walk quietly up Mount Moriah and stand before God to make their reply: "We are."

We can see why God is so moved by their willingness—so moved that he does something for Abraham that he has only done for a handful of people in all of human history: he swears an oath to him:

> And the angel of the LORD called to Abraham a second time from heaven, and said, "By myself I have sworn, says the LORD, because you have done this, and have not withheld your son, your only begotten son, I will indeed bless you, and I will multiply your

seed as the stars of heaven and as the sand which is on the seashore. And your seed shall possess the gate of his enemies, and by your seed shall all the nations of the earth be blessed, because you have obeyed my voice." (Gn 22:15–18)

The word "seed" can mean "child" or "children," that is, it can be either singular or plural. You can plant one seed (singular), or you can spread a great deal of seed (plural) on your field. The meaning of "seed" in the passage above could be either. It could refer to *all* Abraham's descendants or to *one particular* descendant.

The most important line in this amazing sworn blessing to Abraham is the last one: "by your seed shall all the nations of the earth be blessed." This is true in two senses. Blessing is going to come to all the nations through Abraham's descendants, the people of Israel. Yet, the greatest blessing to the world that the people of Israel will give is the one unique "seed" of Abraham, Jesus the Christ. Through this "seed" will come God's Holy Spirit, which is the greatest blessing humanity can enjoy.

Throughout the Bible, "swearing an oath" and "making a covenant" mean almost the same thing, somewhat like "exchanging vows" and "getting married" are almost synonymous. For that reason, we can see in God's great oath to Abraham in Genesis 22:15–18 the final form of God's *covenant* with Abraham, in which the promise of universal blessing to all nations is finally included in the covenant. For that reason, when I have to summarize the history of salvation in just a few images, I focus on Mount Moriah to represent the Abrahamic Covenant.

Mount Moriah is easy to draw:

The altar is just a pile of round stones with Isaac on top:

And Abraham, with the big knife, completes the picture:

From now on, this will be our icon to remember the Abrahamic Covenant.

There's one more thing we should mention about the sacrifice of Isaac. Many years later, Jewish religious leaders considered the question "Why did the sacrifice of animals in the ancient temple cause God to forgive sins?" After all, it's hard to see why killing an animal would forgive human sin. Even the Old Testament seems to say that, by itself, the blood of bulls and goats cannot take away sin (Is 1:11, 66:3; Ps 50:8–13).

The Covenant with Abraham

The Jewish tradition concluded that the killing of animals, by itself, could not have meant much to God. No, the sacrifices must have gotten their power from somewhere else. But from where? The answer they came up with was brilliant: from the near-sacrifice of Isaac. Abraham's obedient consent to the death of his only begotten son, and Isaac's willingness to die out of obedience and love—these were things that *did* have real value in God's eyes. Since Isaac's near-sacrifice took place on the very site of the future temple, some rabbis taught that the animal sacrifices were a kind of reminder or *re-presentation* of the one and only, really powerful sacrifice of Isaac.

Does that sound somehow familiar, Catholics? Think about it, next time you go to Mass.

This is how far we have now gotten in salvation history:

Adamic Covenant   Noahic Covenant

Abrahamic Covenant

SELF-STUDY GUIDE

Background

The Abrahamic Covenant is interesting because it is made with a previously anonymous man whom God calls to move from his homeland to a promised land in Canaan. Like Adam and Noah before him, Abraham has doubts. He can't be sure how the covenant promises can come true. In Genesis 12, God makes three specific promises to Abraham, who was then called Abram, and seals them in a ceremony in which he calls down a curse upon himself if he does not fulfill it. As with the other covenants, Abraham takes a step back and falls when he fathers a child with Sarah's maid Hagar. It is then that God renews the covenant and changes his name. The final covenant with Abraham is the most important and a foreshadowing of the covenant God will make with the world with his Son, Jesus Christ. Abraham is asked to sacrifice his son, Isaac. God is so moved by his willingness that he swears an oath to him: Abraham's descendants, or one descendant, Jesus, will be the greatest blessing the world has ever seen.

Reading Comprehension

1. Where is present-day Chaldea?
2. What is the "whole reason the Jews are special"?
3. Among his general blessings to Abram, what were three specific things God promised?
4. What did the covenant ceremony in which the animals were split in two mean? How did it involve divine condescension?

The Covenant with Abraham

5. What are some special promises made to Abram in Genesis 15?
6. What is the "mini-fall" of Abram in Genesis 16?
7. In Genesis 17, how does God add to the promises he makes to Abram in Genesis 15?
8. What are two possible meanings of circumcision as part of the covenant?
9. What is the last and best promise of the final covenant between God and Abraham?
10. Why does the Bible call Abraham a prophet?

Reading in Context

In your notebook, explain the relationship between each of the following pairs of words:

1. Noah, Ham
2. Abram, Chaldean
3. Abram, Abraham
4. Abraham, Sarah
5. Sarah, Hagar
6. Abraham, Hagar
7. Abraham, Ishmael
8. Abraham, Isaac
9. Abraham, Moriah
10. Isaac, Jesus
11. Abraham, God

Writing Assignment

Write two to three paragraphs summarizing the final covenant with Abraham as represented by the drawings from this chapter.

Small-Group Guide

Opening Prayer

Loving Father,

Thank you for this precious gift of your Word, through which we may come to know and worship you more fully and love you more deeply.

Lord Jesus Christ, today we gather as your disciples. We sit at your feet ready to listen to your Word. We humbly ask that you open our ears so that we may hear with our intellect and open our hearts so that we may know you intimately.

Come, Holy Spirit; fill us with your gifts of wisdom, understanding, and knowledge so that we may grow in love, faithfulness, and joy. Amen.

Discussion Questions

1. In this chapter, we see a pattern of God's love for his children. When Adam and Eve fell, he renewed the Covenant with Noah. And then Noah fell, even after God demonstrated his great mercy in saving Noah and his family. Once again, the relationship with God was broken. Once again, God repaired it—this time with Abram, by giving him three blessings and changing his name to Abraham.

   List three blessings God has given you.

2. Identify how Abraham failed to trust in God and his perfect plan. What do you think was at the root of Abraham's decision to follow Sarah's advice and

take Hagar as a wife in order to produce a son? A lack of trust in God? Impatience? Pride? Explain your answer.

Do you have implicit trust in God's plan for you?

3. The story of Abraham and Sarah reflects more closely our modern experience. We're not given a garden paradise to tend or a charge to build an ark. Instead, we are given a simple command to trust the Lord and his unique plan for us.

How can you apply this lesson in trusting the Lord and his plan to your life?

4. Abraham and Sarah took matters into their own hands instead of waiting for God's perfect plan. The result was strife for not only Abraham and Sarah but also Hagar.

Waiting for God's timing is not a recent invention. Examine a time in your life when you felt God wasn't acting quickly enough, and you acted to get something. How did that play out? How did you feel? What did that do to your relationship with God?

5. God gave Abraham an opportunity to repair their relationship. God asked Abraham to sacrifice his only son, Isaac. This was the ultimate sacrifice of his only son (and foreshadowed God's sacrifice of his only begotten Son). Abraham's willingness to trust God now, with higher stakes, was duly noted by God.

We often make sacrifices for those we love. Can you approach these sacrifices with detachment as an offering for God? How does spiritual detachment release you from holding onto your will and open you to God's will?

Bonus: In your notebook, draw a stick figure of yourself, joyful in your role as child of God. Add a symbol of one of God's blessings for you.

Closing Prayer

Faithful Father,

Thank you for your unconditional love. We are grateful for the many blessings you have poured out for us, seen and unseen.

We praise you and glorify you in word and deed as we strive to love and trust you unconditionally. Bless us in our endeavor to live fully your teachings. Amen.

FOUR
GOD'S LAWS, ISRAEL'S FLAWS
The Covenant through Moses

Suggested Reading: Exodus 1-20, 24, 32-34, 40

The Long Story from Abraham to Moses
(Genesis 23-Exodus 1)

When we left Abraham at the end of the last chapter, he had just gotten a solemn oath from God that confirmed all the promises God had ever made to him. Abraham knew he would become a great nation, receive a "great name," and become a blessing to the whole world.

The only problem was that it would take some time. God had said so back in Genesis 15:13. As the story continues from Genesis 23 to Exodus 1, everything plays out as God had predicted that dark night when he first made the "covenant of the pieces" with Abraham. Abraham's grandson Jacob, whose name is later changed to Israel, ends up with twelve sons, and his sons are quite prolific. The whole clan of them end up moving to Egypt because of a famine and a crazy mix-up that began with an attempt to sell their brother Joseph into slavery. The living is good in Egypt, so they stay there permanently—well, for about four hundred years, to be exact. That's a long time—much longer than the United States has been an independent nation.

What was God doing with the people of Israel for all that time? What about the promises to Abraham?

Actually, this long time was necessary for God to fulfill his promises to Abraham. A nation isn't born overnight. The tribes of Israel needed time to grow. In Egypt, with its mighty Nile river and fertile fields, the people of Israel had plenty of food and safety, and grew to be very numerous.

Nothing's Perfect *(Exodus 2)*

There was just one problem with this pleasant scenario. The Israelites ended up as slaves of the Egyptians. As they say, nothing's perfect.

At first it seems the situation of slavery was fairly mild, but it became increasingly harsh as the Egyptians felt increasingly threatened by these fertile foreigners in their land. The Bible says the Israelites "groaned under their bondage, and cried out for help. . . . And God heard their groaning, and God remembered his covenant with Abraham, with Isaac, and with Jacob" (Ex 2:23–24).

So God set in motion his plan to take his people out of Egypt.

It began, like most of God's plans, with the birth of a child. This child was named Moses, and the Bible says he was a "special child" (Ex 2:2). The Bible doesn't say how they knew he was special. The Dead Sea Scrolls record a (somewhat humorous) tradition that Moses's ancestor Noah glowed brightly at birth. Maybe Moses inherited the same gene!

In any event, Moses's mother had to hide him because Pharoah had decided to kill Hebrew baby boys. When Moses was too big to be hidden any longer, his mother put him in a basket and floated him down the Nile. This was the ancient equivalent of leaving a baby on someone's doorstep. Hopefully, someone would find the baby floated up on the shore and take him home to care for him. We know of other examples of people doing this in ancient times. This ploy could be especially effective in Egypt, because the Nile was a god. Whoever found the baby might think it was a gift of the Nile god.

I don't need to retell the whole story of the Exodus because you've probably seen DreamWorks's movie *Prince of Egypt* already, which isn't half bad in terms of getting across the main points of the story. There are just a few points I would want to make.

First, the plan to float the baby down the Nile paid off *incredibly* well. The baby gets adopted by the richest girl in Egypt, Pharoah's daughter. Moses's biological mom gets paid by the government to nurse her own baby. And Moses is in line to rise in the royal court until he is in a position to influence state policy toward the Hebrews and get them released. In hindsight, we can say that was probably God's "Plan A" for freeing Israel. All Moses had to do was stay put and stay out of trouble until he had the power to free his people legally. That's "how it should have ended."

But no, *of course* Moses had to mess up the plan. He gets hotheaded and kills an Egyptian who's beating up one of his fellow Hebrews. Then he buries the body in sand (Ex 2:11–12).

How smart was that? We want to say: "Moses, throw the body in the trunk of a chariot and drive it off a bridge into the Nile or something! But bury it in *sand?* What are you thinking?"

As expected, the sand blows off, the body is found, Moses is discovered, and he has to flee to the far side of the desert to get away from his adopted grandfather the Pharaoh (Ex 2:13–15). He ends up tending sheep for a living (Ex 3:1). This is the ancient equivalent of sweeping floors or flipping burgers. He was raised a prince of Egypt, and Egyptians considered shepherding so disgusting that they wouldn't even eat with such people (Gn 46:34). What a fall from the White House to the out-house!

Forty years of shepherding later, Moses is already an old man, and we can imagine his memories of Egypt and his palace upbringing have faded with time. Apparently, he has no future and no ambition left, except to stay alive and live out his life with his wife and son.

The Burning Bush *(Exodus 3)*

But at this point, God once again intervenes in Moses's life. Appearing in the form of a burning bush, God shows himself to Moses and reveals to him the secret of his name. Now, names don't mean too much to modern Americans. When we find out we're going to have a baby, we get a book of baby names and try to choose something that sounds good.

"Robert?"

"No, too plain, and everyone will call him Bob."

"Dean?"

"There was a kid in fifth grade I didn't like named Dean."

"How about Aidan?"

"The Johnsons just named their baby Aidan, and we'll look like we're copying."

As Americans, we're into the sound of names, but we're not as much concerned with their *meaning*. The ancient Israelites were quite the opposite. The sound meant nothing—the *meaning* of the name was everything, because the

The Covenant through Moses

name represented the person. In a mysterious way, the name expressed the *reality* of the person.

So it is a dramatic moment when Moses says, "If they ask me 'what is his name,' what shall I say?" and God responds, "I AM WHO I AM." Say, 'I AM' has sent me to you" (Ex 3:13–14).

By saying this, God identifies himself as the one God who actually exists; all other gods are fake, they ARE NOT. But God IS.

The actual name given to Moses for the Israelites to use in praying to God was not exactly the phrase "I AM" but rather a word that probably meant "HE IS." In Hebrew, it is spelled YHWH. In some old Bibles you will find it written as "Jehovah," but that name resulted from a series of pronunciation mistakes through history and is not how it ever sounded in ancient times. In almost all Catholic Bibles in English, whenever God's special name "YHWH" (literally, "HE IS!") is used, you will find the name "LORD" in capitals. The Catholic Church generally follows the ancient Jewish practice of saying "LORD" rather than pronouncing the holy name.

After revealing his name to Moses, God commissions him: "You shall say to Pharaoh, Israel is my first-born son, and I say to you, Let my son go that he may serve me" (Ex 4:22–23). This reminds us of Adam, the firstborn son of God. It is almost as though God is adopting the Israelites as a new Adam, a new humanity.

Let's draw an Israelite:

And make his face shine because as firstborn son he reflects the glory of God the Father:

When God says to Pharaoh, "Let my son go that he may *serve* me," that word "serve" in Hebrew is often used of *worship*, just as in English we speak of "worship *services*." We could just as well translate God's message as "let my son go that he may *worship* me." This points to a priestly status for the people of Israel. They are going to be a people dedicated to the *worship* of God.

Pharaoh, unfortunately, is not pleased with Moses's message from the LORD. Like the CEO of any large corporation, he is not much inclined to let his cheap labor leave for an indefinite vacation, even if it is part of their religion. So Pharaoh's very predictable answer is "No!", and in fact he increases everyone's workload to discourage any future efforts to negotiate a better labor contract (Ex 5:4–21).

The Rout of the Gods *(Exodus 7–14)*

The stage is set, then, for a "battle of the gods." That's what the ten plagues really are, after all (Ex 7–11). Pharaoh himself was considered a god by the Egyptians, and for whatever Pharaoh couldn't handle, there was an entire crew of other Egyptian gods that "had his back." These included Hapi, the Nile god; Hekhet, the frog goddess; and Amon-Re, the sun god. The ten plagues were contests between the Lord, God of the slaves, and the gods of the Egyptians (Ex 12:12; Nm 33:4). However, the gods of the Egyptians start losing about one minute into the first quarter, and it's a total rout for the rest of the game.

HOME GODS	VISITOR GOD
0	10
Final	

Recap: First, Hapi, the Nile god, is slain, and all the water of the Nile turns to blood (Ex 7:20–24). Then Hekhet, the frog goddess of fertility, gets out of hand and becomes *way* overly fertile (Ex 8:1–6). And so it continues, one so-called god after another is made to look ridiculous and powerless. Even Amon-Re, the almighty sun god, is locked in the dark for three days (Ex 10:21–23). Finally, it's proven that Pharaoh himself is no god, as he is unable to save his own son's life in the final plague (Ex 12:29–32).

God was teaching the Egyptians that their religion was false, and that they ought to worship him instead. Many of the Egyptians eventually got the point (Ex 9:20). After the last plague, Pharaoh himself gave up and let the Israelites leave the land (Ex 12:32).

The Route of the Israelites *(Exodus 15-19)*

Even then, the drama was far from over. As soon as Moses had led the Israelites to the shores of the Red Sea, Pharaoh changed his mind yet again and sent his army out after them. Once more, God engaged in divine combat, moving his fiery presence between the Egyptians and the Israelites while the Hebrews escaped through a divided sea that crashed together over the pursuing soldiers (Ex 15).

Once the Israelites were safely across the sea and in the desert, their enemies were no longer the Egyptians but basic hunger and thirst. So God caused water to spring out of the rocks and rained down a mysterious substance from heaven, so unusual the Hebrews asked, "Man-hu?" (that is, "What is it?"). So it's name became *man,* which means "what?" in Hebrew, but in English we usually say *manna* (Ex 16).

At last, the Israelites reached their destination: Sinai, the very mountain where, years earlier, God had spoke to Moses out of the burning bush (Ex 19). Here we want to slow the story down a little to make a couple of key points.

God has brought the Israelites, under Moses, out to Sinai to make a covenant with them. We've already seen that a covenant is a family bond. God told Pharaoh, "Israel is my

The Covenant through Moses

First-Born Son" (Ex 4:22), so it seems God's purpose in this Sinai covenant is to adopt Israel formally into that *filial relationship*.

God makes a striking promise to Israel just before he appears in all his fearsome glory on Sinai to give them the Ten Commandments. God says, "If you will obey my voice and keep my covenant . . . you shall be to me a *royal priesthood and a holy nation*" (Ex 19:5–6).

The picture is becoming clearer. As a group, the Israelites are a new Adam. God is adopting them into sonship and giving them a royal (kingly) and priestly status. So we can take our shining Israelite,

and clothe him with a stole and crown,

at which point he's beginning to look a lot like Adam—which is the point, of course.

So does this mean God has no plan for the rest of humanity? No. God does not say, "Israel is my only son." He says "Israel is my *first-born* son." That implies that the other nations are younger sons of God (Dt 32:8).

Moreover, priests need laypeople to serve, and kings need subjects to rule. So when God says to Israel, "You will be a royal priesthood," he suggests that the rest of the world, the other nations, are going to be the laity and subjects that the Israelites will rule and serve. This was God's "Plan A" for the Israelites.

The Covenant at Sinai *(Exodus 20-24)*

That was the plan, but it had to be put into practice. God's awesome presence descended on Mount Sinai.

The Covenant through Moses

Exodus describes an earthquake, fire, darkness, a cloud, smoke, and lightning surrounding the mountain:

In Exodus 20, Moses goes up on the mount, and God gives him the Ten Commandments, written on tablets of stone. As a result of being in God's presence, Moses's face began to glow (Ex 34:29–30). To illustrate Moses, we're going to give him two beams of light coming from his face (Ex 34:35).

But this picture is a little complicated, so we're going to simplify it a bit to get the icon for the Mosaic Covenant, when God tried to restore to Israel the *filial relationship* that Adam once enjoyed:

What was the purpose of the Ten Commandments? Every family has to have rules. I have a big family (seven kids still at home), and we have lots of rules. Most of them are written out and taped to the center of all family life: the refrigerator. I imagine that, if we were to adopt a child into our family, one of the first things we would have to do would be to take him or her to the refrigerator and explain the basic family rules.

At Sinai, God is adopting Israel as his "firstborn son." The Ten Commandments are the family rules. The first three rules govern the relationship with the Father. The next seven govern relationships with fellow siblings—other human beings.

BEHAVING TOWARD YOUR FATHER	BEHAVING TOWARD YOUR SIBLINGS
You shall have no other gods besides me.	Honor your father and mother.
Do not misuse the Name of God.	Do not kill.
Keep the Sabbath day holy.	Do not commit adultery.
	Do not steal.
	Do not lie.
	Do not covet anyone's spouse.
	Do not covet anyone's possessions.

The next three chapters of Exodus (21–23) give the Israelites additional rules derived from the Ten Commandments, rules intended to govern their life as a nation. After all, the Israelites are not only a family but also a nation with a government and civil laws.

The story in Exodus 24 once again emphasizes the sonship of Israel to God. Moses goes to the foot of Mount Sinai and builds an altar there. Then, with the help of some mysterious "young men" from the people of Israel—more about them later—he offers sacrifices to God. Then he reads all the commandments—the "family rules"—to the people. "All that the LORD has spoken, we will do!" cry the Israelites (Ex 24:3–7).

Afterward, Moses takes half of the blood of the sacrifices and sprinkles it on the people, and half of the blood he throws against the altar. The altar represented God's presence. Throwing the blood on the altar *and* on the people meant they now *shared one blood.* God and the people were now family!

But the ritual also had a darker meaning: if either party were to break the covenant, *may his blood be shed.* Moses ends the ceremony with solemn words: "Behold, the blood of the covenant which the LORD has made with you!" (Ex 24:8).

Families eat together. At least they ought to, although between soccer practice, music lessons, and TV, who has the time anymore? But certainly in ancient times (that is, before organized sports), families used to eat together. That's why, as soon as the "one blood" ceremony is over, God invites Moses and the leaders of the people up Mount Sinai to share a meal with him. The Bible says, "They saw God, and ate and drank" (Ex 24:11).

Now the family-making ceremonies are concluded. God has not been so close to human beings since Adam and Eve were expelled from the Garden. The Garden once served as the place where God could meet and talk with his children. The children of Israel are going to need a new "Eden" where they can meet with God—and it would help if this "Eden" were portable because, as you can see, they are currently wandering around in a desert. So God brings Moses back up Mount Sinai to get instructions for the Tabernacle, a big tent for meeting God, decorated with reminders of Eden (Ex 25–31).

This is the honeymoon of the people of Israel with God. Everything is good. Everything has finally worked out.

But the honeymoon doesn't last long.

The End of the Honeymoon *(Exodus 32–34)*

It would be nice if the story of Israel and God ended here: they have become family, and they live happily ever after. Israel has the status of firstborn son and royal priest among the nations. We don't know exactly how that would have worked out, but presumably they would have ruled among the other

The Covenant through Moses

peoples of the earth and led the other nations in worship, so that the "younger sons"—the other peoples—could also enter into God's family.

Of course, that's not what happened. Moses was up on the mountain getting instructions for the Tabernacle too long—or so the Israelites thought. Figuring he was "missing in action," they decided to abandon this new religion they had adopted and go back to their old religion: bull worship, like they had done in Egypt. They pressured Aaron to make them a golden bull calf. The Bible says they offered sacrifices to this idol, then "sat down to eat and drink, and rose up to play" (Ex 32:6). The word "play" here sounds pretty innocent, but the kinds of things they started doing were in all likelihood not that innocent. Pagan worship was often quite scandalous.

Moses comes down the mountain and is not in the least bit pleased. Smashing the tablets with the Ten Commandments, he rallies his own tribe—the Levites—and imposes martial law to regain control of the people, who had gotten out of hand with the partying. (Think Woodstock, for those of you who remember.)

The Levites went through the camp, fighting and executing the ringleaders of this rebellion. As a result of their courage, Moses promised them the status of priests for Israel (Ex 32:25–29).

The aftermath of the rebellion was not pretty. In Exodus 33–34, Moses goes back up Mount Sinai to plead with God to take Israel back into the covenant. God consents and remakes the covenant with Israel in Exodus 34. But things are not the same. The covenant has been damaged. Although God renews the covenant, it's not as good as it was before. We are going to call this "remake" of the Mosaic Covenant "Second Sinai."

Here's the icon for "Second Sinai." It looks like the original Sinai covenant, but now the tablets are cracked:

If you read the Bible carefully, from Exodus 32 on, you can see that, when God remakes the covenant with Israel, he includes a great many more laws the second time around—for example, the entire Book of Leviticus, with all its laws about sacrifices and staying "clean," is added into the covenant after the golden calf. Let's add some more tablets of law to represent this fact:

Since ancient times, Christians have viewed these additional laws given after the calf as having a *penitential purpose.* When you go to confession, the priest gives you a penance to perform: usually a prayer to say or a good deed to perform. The penance the priest gives is never a bad thing. Nonetheless, he makes you do it because you have sinned.

The extra laws added into the covenant after the calf are similar. They are not bad things to do, but they were assigned to Israel because of Israel's sin. They were meant to teach

The Covenant through Moses

certain spiritual truths. For example, the laws of sacrifice usually involved the killing of an animal (Lv 1–7). This taught the lesson that sin leads to death. Since God is life, turning away from him (which is sin) always means death for someone or something.

So the extra laws taught spiritual lessons and helped restore Israel to spiritual health—which are the same goals as penances have today. St. Paul seems to teach this "penitential" view of the Law in Galatians 3:19, where he states, "Why then the law? It was added because of transgressions."

By the word "law," St. Paul probably does not mean the Ten Commandments. They were not *added* to anything else. They were original. He may be thinking of the great bulk of regulations (like the whole Book of Leviticus) that were *added* later, after the *transgressions* of the calf incident in Exodus 32.

As we continue to read in the Bible, we find that, finally, after an entire year at Mount Sinai, God has given all the additional laws, and Moses has gotten the people organized into marching order for entry into the Promised Land (Nm 1–10).

Desert Deserters: Abandoning God in the Wilderness
(Numbers 1, 10–25)

My older readers will remember a certain TV show called *Gilligan's Island* about castaways shipwrecked on an island for years, after what was supposed to be a "three-hour tour—a *three-hour* tour!" The Israelite trip to the Promised Land turned out to be a little like *Gilligan's Island*. It should've been short, but it ended up lasting a lifetime. To walk from Mount Sinai to the Promised Land should have been a matter of days—weeks at most. Yet they ended up wandering in the desert for *forty years.*

Why? Because of more rebellions. As we read into the Book of Numbers, the people of Israel don't leave Sinai until chapter 10, and they start rebelling against God in the first verse of chapter 11! They complain about everything—the food, the water, and how Moses is running things. At one point or another, everyone gets involved—from the poor folks on the edge of the camp to the high-class and influential Aaron and Miriam, Moses's own siblings. There are, in fact, at least nine rebellions against God recounted in the Book of Numbers. The impression one gets is that the whole forty years of wandering was one long revolt.

One key rebellion we want to focus on takes place in Numbers 14, where the people of Israel send twelve spies into the Promised Land to scout it out. These spies were a pessimistic bunch and bring back a bad report: "We are not able to go up against the Canaanites; for they are stronger than we!" (Nm 13:31). The people panic, lose their faith, and want to kill Moses and choose someone else to lead them back to Egypt.

In a repeat of the golden calf event, Moses finds himself once again pleading with God on behalf of the people. Again, the LORD relents and forgives the people in response to Moses's prayers. But God insists the current generation will die while wandering in the desert, and only their children will enter into the Promised Land.

The second generation—the children of those who left Egypt—grow up in the desert from Numbers 14 through 24. We have high hopes for them, especially after they are blessed four times by a certain prophet named Balaam (Nm 22–24). But our hopes are crushed when the second generation also falls into the trap of worshiping pagan gods, at a place called "Beth Peor" in the land of Moab, just outside of the Promised Land (Nm 25).

So at the end of Numbers, things are pretty low. The people of Israel have been rebelling against God for forty years in the wilderness. The second generation has grown up, but they are not much better than their parents. If it wasn't for Moses's efforts, the LORD and Israel would have parted ways long ago.

Deuteronomy, One Long Homily
(Deuteronomy 5-9, 31-34)

At this juncture, we have a final remaking of the covenant through Moses. This remaking is called Deuteronomy. The word "Deuteronomy" actually comes from the Greek words *deutero* meaning "second," and *nomos*, meaning "law." The Deuteronomy is the "second law." Actually, it's the "third law" if we are very strict about it, but the ancient folks who compiled the Bible for us lumped first and second Sinai together and counted two law-givings: Sinai and Deuteronomy.

It is important to remember that what happens in the Book of Deuteronomy is very different than what happened at Sinai. The events at Sinai took place within a year after the Exodus (Nm 10:11–12). Deuteronomy takes place forty years after the Exodus (Dt 1:3). The Sinai events occurred on or near the famous mountain; Deuteronomy takes place in the land of Moab, a flat area just outside the land of Israel to the east (Dt 1:5).

At Sinai, God appeared to the people in thunder, cloud, and lightning. In Deuteronomy, God does not appear to the people at all. He does speak privately with Moses, but all the people see is Moses preaching to them, for thirty-four chapters! How's that for a long-winded homily?

Moreover, for much of the time, Moses is not in a good mood (Dt 1:37, 3:26, 31:24–29):

The Covenant through Moses

He reminds the people of all the times they broke the covenant and rebelled against God (Dt 9:1–29, 32:1–47):

Then he gives them the laws of the covenant *again,* this time adding yet *more* laws, including some that were not so great (Dt 12–26). As Jesus will point out well over a thousand years later, some of the laws Moses gives in Deuteronomy weren't God's best laws but were given because of the "hardness of heart" of the Israelites (Mt 19:8; compare Ez 20:25; Gal 3:19).

The best example is the law on divorce. Divorce is not mentioned in the laws of Sinai. But in Deuteronomy, after forty years of rebellion in the wilderness, Moses quietly allows the men of Israel to divorce their wives (Dt 24:1). This was not God's highest and best law, but it may have been impractical to hold these men to a higher standard.

Another example would be the laws on warfare. In Deuteronomy, Moses forbids the Israelites to make any peace treaties with the people in the Promised Land (Dt 20:16–18). They have to fight a total war against them. This is not the highest and best way, either. However, Moses fears that anything less than total war will result in the Israelites getting sucked into the pagan ways of the people of the land (Dt 20:18). Unfortunately, his fears turned out to be well founded. The people ended up not waging a total war, and eventually they did adopt the paganism of the Canaanites (Jgs 3:5–6).

Nonetheless, for better or worse, Deuteronomy became the third and final making of the covenant through Moses. The Book of Deuteronomy became the final form of the Law of the covenant for the people of Israel for the rest of their existence.

After giving the laws of Deuteronomy, Moses climbs a certain Mount Pisgah in the land of Moab, and God gives him a view of the entire Promised Land (Dt 34:1–8). Then, he dies. Some say he was buried by God; others, that God assumed his body to heaven. Sadly, he never completed his mission to bring the Israelites into their homeland.

In any event, the end of Deuteronomy concludes the books of Moses and the biblical account of the Mosaic Covenant. As we've seen, this covenant is a little complicated. It's broken and remade at least twice:

First Sinai   Second Sinai   Deuteronomy

The Covenant through Moses

For our purposes, we'll concentrate on first Sinai when we have to list the covenant of Moses with the other covenants of salvation history:

So far, then, we've learned four of these:

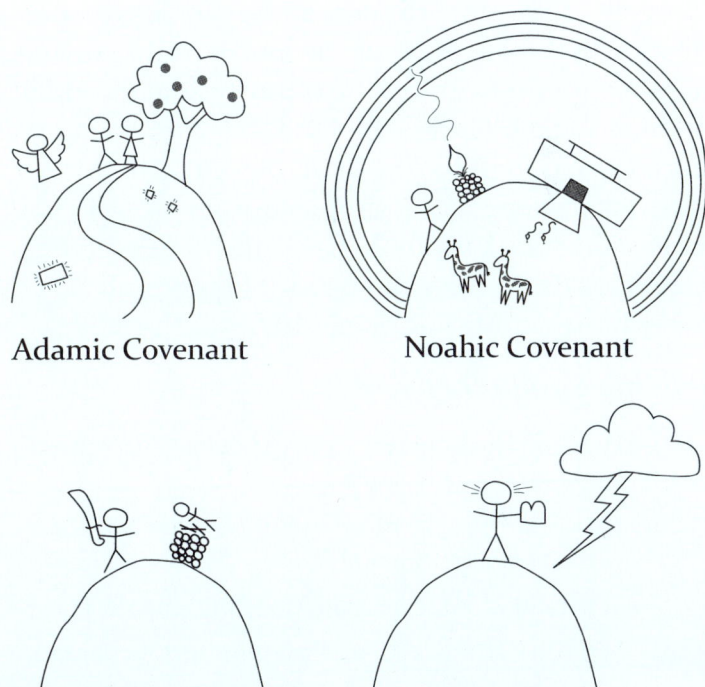

Adamic Covenant

Noahic Covenant

Abrahamic Covenant

Mosaic Covenant

Self-Study Guide

Background

The Mosaic Covenant, like the other covenants discussed thus far, is multifaceted with many starts and stops due mainly to the stubbornness and sinfulness of the Israelites. This chapter begins with Moses's early life and his loss of the Pharaoh's goodwill after he murdered a slave owner and buried him in the sand. After he meets God and receives his mission to free Israel from Egyptian slavery, God reveals his power over the false gods of Egypt. In the desert, the people grumble against Moses and the difficulty of the journey immediately. They do celebrate God's gift of the commandments and promise in blood to be one with the Lord, but they soon break this promise. Through Moses, God offers a series of extra laws designed as penance. A simple journey from Egypt to the Promised Land that should have taken weeks actually takes forty years due to several revolts by the people. Eventually, due to Moses's fortitude, Israel arrives at the foot of Canaan.

Reading Comprehension

1. How did the long stay in Egypt help the people of Israel grow as a nation?
2. How did Moses's mom's plan to spare her baby work out incredibly well?
3. What did Moses eventually do to mess up the plan?
4. Why do Catholics generally honor the Jewish practice of not saying God's special name Yhwh?

The Covenant through Moses

5. In what other way can God's words to Pharaoh—"Let my son go that he may serve me"—be translated from the Hebrew?
6. What happened in the "battle of the gods"?
7. What was God's purpose in the final Sinai covenant?
8. When God says, "Israel is my first-born son," what does this imply?
9. What was the purpose of the Ten Commandments?
10. What was the purpose of the "second Sinai" covenant?
11. Why did the Israelites have to stay in the desert for forty years?
12. What does Moses do in the Book of Deuteronomy?
13. Redraw the book's sketches for the Adamic Covenant, the Noahic Covenant, the Abrahamic Covenant, and the Mosaic Covenant.

Reading in Context

In your notebook, fill in the blanks with the terms from this chapter listed below. You will not use every term.

Jacob	Mount Sinai	Moab	Pharaoh	Jews
Hapi	Sarah	manna	Levites	Mount Moriah
Miriam	Egypt	Mount Pisgah	YHWH	Tabernacle

1. The mysterious substance that the Israelites ate in the desert was called "_____."

2. _____ was Moses's sister.

3. _____ was Moses's adopted grandfather.

4. The _____ was a big tent for meeting God that was decorated with reminders of Eden.

5. Moses's own tribe, the _____, were priests of Israel.

6. The Nile god, _____, was slain, and all the water of the river turned to blood.

7. On _____, God gave Moses the Ten Commandments.

8. _____ later took the name Israel.

9. Deuteronomy takes place in the land of _____, an area just outside of the land of Israel.

10. Before he died, Moses climbed _____ and was able to view the entire Promised Land.

Drawing and Writing Assignment

Draw the first Sinai, second Sinai, and Deuteronomy covenants in your notebook and write a one-paragraph explanation of each under each drawing.

Small-Group Guide

Opening Prayer

Loving Father,

Thank you for this precious gift of your Word, through which we may come to know and worship you more fully and love you more deeply.

Lord Jesus Christ, today we gather as your disciples. We sit at your feet ready to listen to your Word. We humbly ask that you open our ears so that we may hear with our intellect and open our hearts so that we may know you intimately.

Come, Holy Spirit; fill us with your gifts of wisdom, understanding, and knowledge so that we may grow in love, faithfulness, and joy. Amen.

Discussion Questions

1. God's promise to Abraham was kept; Abraham did indeed become the father of nations.

   His descendants, however, became enslaved in Egypt, and God sent Moses to free them. Through Moses we received the Ten Commandments and other rules for leading holy and virtuous lives.

   Recall your early catechism training: list the Ten Commandments.

2. Identify the commandments that order our relationship with God, the Father. Identify the commandments that order our behavior toward each other, our brothers and sisters.

3. The Ten Commandments are specific to certain behaviors but also have a broad application. For example, "Thou shall not kill" is very clear about prohibiting murder, but there are broader applications of this commandment. It also applies to not killing (destroying) a person's spirit as well as to other ways we can wound or kill someone metaphorically.

   Do you consciously apply these rules for living a faithful life? Do you have a regular examination of conscience? How could you introduce this into your weekly or daily routine?

4. The story of the Israelite people in the desert shows us the depth of God's love for his people even as they continue to disappoint him through their sinful behavior. The Israelites suffer for their sinfulness, yet God condescends, time and again, to offer them a new covenant. God does not give up on them, and, finally, they give themselves over to God's laws and the remade covenant.

   How do we express our rebellion against God's law today? Our society is rife with examples, but also look interiorly as you consider this question.

5. Our heavenly Father is a loving and just God. We have seen that there are consequences to our disobedience. In his mercy, God has provided not only the Ten Commandments but also other practices that help us achieve and sustain lives of holiness.

   What practice (or devotion) have you integrated into your spiritual life that has borne fruit?

Bonus: In your notebook, draw a stick figure of yourself, joyful in your role as child of God. Add a symbol of a devotion or practice that helps you grow in holiness.

Closing Prayer

Merciful Father,

Thank you for your guidance. We are grateful for the steadfast love you have shown us, even as we have rebelled against you.

We praise you and glorify you in word and deed as we strive to align our wills and hearts to your great plan for us. Bless us in our endeavor to live fully your teachings. Amen.

FIVE
ONCE AND FUTURE KING
The Covenant of David

Suggested Reading: 1 Samuel 16-24; 2 Samuel 5-12, 23

Tribes in Trouble: From Joshua to David

A lot of water flows under the bridge after the giving of the Mosaic Covenant before we have the next big step forward in the history of salvation. About five hundred years pass, according to the biblical chronology.

The Bible chronicles this period of time in the books of Joshua, Judges, Ruth, and 1 Samuel. Personally, I love the stories and lessons contained in these books, which are by turns funny, touching, and even shocking—but never dull. Unfortunately, we only have space to quickly summarize the period.

In the Book of Joshua, we learn how Moses's successor Joshua successfully leads the People of Israel into the Promised Land. Joshua's name in Hebrew is "Y'shua." In the Greek language, this name will come out as "Jesus." Joshua, Moses's successor, is a picture or *type* of a certain Y'shua to come. Like Joshua before him, this later Y'shua will succeed where Moses failed and lead God's people to a place where Moses and his covenant could not take them.

In the Book of Judges, we learn that, after Joshua and his generation passes away, the people of Israel are plunged into turmoil for several hundred years. They fall into a cycle of *sin* against God, *suffering* under their enemies, *sorrow* for their sin, *salvation* under a God-sent leader, and then the cycle of *sin–suffering–sorrow–salvation* repeats itself. Each time God sends them a leader or "judge" who guides the people back to obedience to God and victory over their enemies. Unfortunately, after the death of each judge, the people lapse into disobedience toward God's covenant (Jgs 2:11–23).

The First Book of Samuel begins a long account of the last judge, a certain prophet by the name of Samuel, who oversees a very important transition for the people of Israel: a change in government from *judges* to *kings.* Judges are rulers who lead during their own lifetime, but a *king* passes his leadership role on to his son. This creates a *dynasty,* a series of rulers from one family.

By the time we reach 1 Samuel 8, the people of Israel are tired of the ups and downs of being ruled by judges. They want the stability of having a king. The prophet Samuel warns them that having a king is not all that it is cracked up to be. Having a king also means high taxes and political oppression. However, the people insist on it. Samuel gives in and appoints a king for them: a certain Saul from the tribe of Benjamin.

Saul certainly looks the part: he's a head taller than most other Israelites. Being physically impressive was a big advantage in a day when one of the king's main duties was to lead the army in battle. Saul's reign starts off well enough, but after a couple of military victories, the wheels begin coming off his administration. Saul has too many character flaws. He makes decisions out of fear or without thinking. He's careless about the worship of God. He's insecure, envious, and threatened by the successes of those under him. It soon becomes obvious to Samuel that the people need a different sort of king. So, at this point in the biblical story, we are introduced to the most important man in the Old Testament: David.

Dearest David

The name "David" in Hebrew means "beloved one," and the meaning of David's name is very appropriate to his role in salvation history. David became the "beloved one" of God, and he also became Israel's most beloved king and poet.

It's hard to overestimate the importance of David in the history of salvation. Some think that Moses is the dominant figure of the Old Testament—and no doubt, Moses is an *extremely* important man. However, Moses is mentioned a little over eight hundred times in the Catholic Old Testament, and about 90 percent of those references are in the first six books: Genesis through Joshua. After that, Moses is mentioned only occasionally in the remaining forty books of the Old Testament.

By contrast, David is not mentioned at all in the first seven books of the Bible (Genesis through Judges). We hear of him for the first time at the end of the Book of Ruth, a love story concerning David's great-grandparents, Boaz and Ruth of Bethlehem. After the Book of Ruth, we don't hear of him again until 1 Samuel 16. But after that, it's no contest: David is mentioned *well over a thousand times* in the rest of the Old Testament.

As I tell my students, Genesis through Joshua is "The Moses Channel." But from Ruth to the end of the Old

Testament, it switches to "The David Channel: All David, All the Time." The historical books record the history of the kingdom of David. The psalms were written or inspired by David. The wisdom books flow from Solomon, David's son. The prophets promise David's kingdom will come again.

What's So Great about David?
(1 Samuel 16-17; 2 Samuel 5-6)

You wouldn't necessarily guess that David was destined for greatness when he first appears on the biblical stage. In 1 Samuel 16, Saul's administration has become a mess and is only getting worse. Samuel, on a mission from God, goes to the town of Bethlehem (literally, "House of Bread") to look for a new king. He picks the family of a certain Jesse, a wealthy owner of flocks, and examines his sons for their king potential. None of them seems quite right, until Jesse calls in his last and eighth son, David, who had been out tending the sheep. He's reddish and handsome. God tells Samuel, "This is the one. Anoint him" (1 Sm 16:12). So Samuel does. Eight is sometimes considered the biblical number of a new beginning. With the anointing of David, a new day has dawned in salvation history. At the risk of using big words, I'd like to summarize David's greatness in three categories: *political, liturgical,* and *eschatological ("es-CAT-oh" + "logical")*. In simpler language, David was great for what he did for Israel as a historic nation (*politics*), what he did for worship (*liturgy*), and what he symbolized for the future of God's people (*eschatology*).

Politically, David was a skillful warrior and brilliant general who unified the Twelve Tribes of Israel and laid the foundation not simply of a great nation, but of an Israelite Empire that included the surrounding Gentile nations as satellites

The Covenant of David

or subject states (2 Sm 9). This empire reached its greatest height under David's son Solomon, but Solomon was building on the momentum left from his father (1 Kgs 10).

One of David's first and most strategic moves was to establish Jerusalem as the capital of Israel (2 Sm 5). Jerusalem was a city that had never been captured and held by any of the tribes of Israel. Down to David's day, Jerusalem remained controlled by a people known as the Jebusites, original inhabitants of the land whom the Israelites were unable to drive out.

Jerusalem also lay on the boundary between the Israelite North and South. To the north of Jerusalem lay the land of the northern Ten Tribes. To the south of Jerusalem lay the large southern territory of the tribe of Judah (which had long since absorbed the tribe of Simeon as well). This was the major cultural divide of Israel. It was the Israelite "Mason-Dixon Line."

Since Jerusalem had not previously belonged to any Israelite tribe, David was not taking any tribe's territory away by making it his capital. Furthermore, since it was on the border of North and South, he was favoring neither the northern tribes nor his own southern tribe by placing his capital there. David's move was politically brilliant, and very much like America's decision to place her capital in Washington, DC, or Canada's choice of Ottawa (on the border of Ontario and Quebec).

In later history, Jerusalem became (and remains) the greatest city of Israel. In fact, we can scarcely imagine Judaism, Christianity, or the Bible itself without Jerusalem at the center. However, we need to keep in mind that Moses *said nothing about Jerusalem.* In fact, Jerusalem is scarcely mentioned in the Bible before David makes it his capital in 2 Samuel 5. After that, however, it's mentioned about *eight hundred times.* Every time we hear "Jerusalem," we need to remember David. Without David, there would be no Jerusalem.

Liturgically, David was a great reformer who personally "practiced what he preached" by modeling for his people the important place that worship should have in their lives. David's second act as king—after making Jerusalem his capital—was to bring the Ark of the Covenant up into his new capital (2 Sm 6). The Ark of the Covenant was a kind of portable throne for God's presence, made by Moses to serve as the center for the worship of God's people. David's intention in bringing the Ark up to Jerusalem was to make it convenient for himself (as the king) to worship God and also to place divine worship at the center of national life.

But David did more for worship than move the Ark to his capital. He also introduced singing and music into worship for the first time. That's right: all of Moses's worship took place in silence. Singing songs and hymns to God while worshipping was a novelty introduced by David. In ancient Israel, a sacred song was a *mizmor,* translated into Greek as a *psalmos,* which gives us our English word "psalm" and the Book of Psalms. David was the first writer of psalms. According to the biblical tradition, most of the psalms passed down to us were written by David or by men he appointed to sing in the sanctuary. David is remembered as the "sweet singer of Israel" (2 Sm 23:1). The Psalms he wrote speak of the intense relationship he had with God. The high priority David placed on worship is certainly one of the reasons the Bible calls him "a man after God's own heart" (1 Sm 13:14).

Finally, David was *a sign of one to come.* David foreshadowed Jesus Christ. The word *christ* is from the Greek translation of the Hebrew word *messiah,* which means "anointed," or literally, "smeared with oil." Like Jesus after him, David is an "anointed one" who is covered not only with oil but also with God's Spirit. This "anointing" by God's Spirit gave David the power to cast out demons (1 Sm 16:13–23). This is why, so many years later, when Jesus casts out demons, people say, "Can this man be the Son of David?" (Mt 12:23).

Like Jesus, David was a *suffering king* for much of his life. Although anointed, David spent most of his early career on the run from his father-in-law King Saul, who persecuted him shamelessly (1 Sm 18–31). Even after becoming king himself, David would later be forced out of office by his son Absalom, who plotted not only to overthrow him but also to kill him (1 Sm 15–20). David wrote about his sufferings in the Psalms, and many of these Psalms became prophecies of the sufferings that Jesus himself would undergo so many years later (see Ps 22).

The Davidic Covenant *(2 Samuel 7)*

From another perspective, we might say David was so important in the Bible because God made a very special covenant with him. In 2 Samuel 7, we see how God ended up granting this covenant to David. David had just become king of all twelve tribes of Israel and made his capital in Jerusalem. David began to feel badly that he himself was living in a lavish palace while God's ark was in a simple tent. He hit on the idea of building a magnificent temple for the ark and told his close friend, the prophet Nathan, about it. Nathan received the following famous reply from the LORD:

> But that same night the word of the LORD came to Nathan, "Go and tell my servant David, 'Thus says the LORD: Would you build me a house to dwell in?' . . . Now therefore thus you shall say to my servant David, 'Thus says the LORD of hosts, I took you from the pasture, from following the sheep, that you should be prince over my people Israel. . . . And I will make for you *a great name,* like the name of the great ones of the earth. . . .

> Moreover the LORD declares to you that the LORD will make you a house. When your days are fulfilled and you lie down with your fathers, I will raise up your offspring (Hebrew *seed*) after you, who shall come forth from your body, and I will establish his kingdom. He shall build a house for my name, and I will establish the throne of his kingdom for ever. I will be his father, and he shall be my son. When he commits iniquity, I will chasten him with the rod of men, with the stripes of the sons of men; but I will not take my steadfast love from him, as I took it from Saul, whom I put away from before you. And your house and your kingdom shall be made sure for ever before me; your throne shall be established for ever." (2 Sm 7:5-16)

In one sense, God's reply can be summarized as "What? You build *me* a house? No, I build *you* a house!" There is a play on the word "house." "House" can mean "temple," as in the phrase "House of God." Or "house" can mean a ruling family or "dynasty." For example, the royal family of England is known as the "House of Windsor," and the Dutch royal family is the "House of Orange." David wants to build God a "house" (temple), but God promises to build David a "house" (dynasty).

We want to notice several promises God gives to David in this covenant. First, let's take note of the promise of a *great name*. We have not seen this promise since the days of Abraham, when God promised Abraham a *great name* during the covenant of circumcision (Gn 17). There is a strong connection between the Abrahamic Covenant and the Davidic Covenant. God's promise of a *great name* to Abraham—which meant royalty—is now being fulfilled in his "seed," David.

The content of the covenant with David mostly concerns the promise of a son and heir who will continue David's

The Covenant of David

kingdom and build a temple for God. This son is called David's "offspring," or literally, "seed." This is another connection with the Abrahamic Covenant, which was also focused on Abraham's "seed." We are going to find out that the "seed" of Abraham and the "seed" of David end up being the same Person (Mt 1:1).

No less important is God's promise that David's son will be adopted as God's own son: "I will be his father, and he shall be my son" (2 Sm 7:14). We have heard almost nothing about divine sonship (*filiation*) since the Book of Exodus, when God referred to Israel as "my first-born son." But Israel didn't seem to want divine sonship very badly. They preferred worshipping a golden calf. The sonship Israel rejected is now being given to David and his sons.

To summarize the Davidic Covenant, God promises David a son who will (1) build God's temple, (2) be the Son of God, and (3) rule over Israel forever. This covenant is given to David on Mount Zion, the part of Jerusalem where David had his palace. Remarkably, Mount Zion looks rather similar to Eden, Moriah, and Sinai:

Let's draw David on top of the mountain:

Since the Davidic Covenant is so tied up with the Temple, we should add that in as well. The Temple is too big to fit on Zion, so it will need a terrace:

The Temple isn't hard to draw—it was a large rectangular building. We'll put a Star of David on it as his temple. (Historically, though, the Star of David wasn't used until much later):

This will be our basic icon for the Davidic Covenant.

Who Was Heir to the Davidic Covenant?

In 2 Samuel 7, God said to David, "When you lie down with your fathers (in other words, die), I will raise up your *seed* after you, who shall come forth from your body, and I will establish his kingdom." So who is this "seed" or son of David referred to here? Most immediately, it refers to Solomon, who will be David's successor and will build a stone temple for God in Jerusalem. However, the "seed" of David also refers to each of David's "sons" or descendants, who will follow Solomon on the throne for hundreds of years. And finally, the "seed" of

David points to one ultimate Son of David who will literally never die, reign on an eternal throne, and build a temple for God that will last forever.

David's Roles and How the Davidic Covenant Fits into Salvation History

The Davidic Covenant promised that David's son would be the adopted son of God. Psalm 89 makes clear that the same promise applied already to David himself, whom God considered his son: "I have found David, my servant. . . . He shall cry to me, 'You are my Father, my God, and the Rock of my salvation.' And I will make him the first-born, the highest of the kings of the earth" (Ps 89:20–27). This reminds us of Adam and of the promise to Israel. And it should! David is like a new Adam, and he embodies the people of Israel. Let's give him the "filial shine":

Of course, David was appointed King of Israel, so we can add the crown:

It's less well known that David was also a priest. Psalm 110 says of David and his successors, "You are a priest forever, after the order of Melchizedek."

Who was Melchizedek? A little research shows he was a priest-king who ruled over Jerusalem during the time of Abraham. He shows up in Genesis 14:18–20. At that time, Jerusalem was known simply as "Salem." How did David wind up as a priest like Melchizedek? It seems that David became Melchizedek's heir and successor when he took over as king of Jerusalem, Melchizedek's old royal city, somewhat similar to the way that someone becomes Peter's successor when he takes over as Bishop of Rome. All the rights and privileges of Melchizedek fell to David—including Melchizedek's priestly role. That's why we see David doing priestly things like wearing an *ephod* (priestly robe), offering sacrifice, and blessing the people (2 Sm 6), and why it says that "David's sons were priests" (2 Sm 8:18).

David also had the gift of prophecy. He himself was aware of it. He says, "The Spirit of the LORD speaks by me, his word is upon my tongue" (2 Sm 23:2). This prophetic gift was part of the "package" when he received the Holy Spirit as a young boy. For this reason, many of the Psalms of David are not only worship songs but prophecies. One of the most famous is Psalm 22, which is easily recognized as a prophecy of the crucifixion:

> My God, my God, why have you forsaken me? . . . All who see me mock at me, they make mouths at me, they wag their heads; "He committed his cause to the LORD; let him deliver him, let him rescue him, for he delights in him!" . . . Yes, dogs are round about me; a company of evildoers encircle me; they have pierced my hands and feet—I can count all my bones—they stare and gloat over me; they divide my garments among them, and for my raiment they cast lots. (Ps 22:1, 7–8, 16–18)

So let's make David a prophet, too:

Finally, David was a sort of bridegroom for the people of Israel. We see a hint of this in a couple of places in the Bible. Most importantly, when the people of Israel come to David to make him king (2 Sm 5), they say to him, "Behold, we are your *bone* and *flesh*," which calls to mind Adam's words about Eve: "Bone of my bone and flesh of my flesh, she shall be called woman" (Gn 2:23). The elders of Israel then make a *covenant* with David to be their king. Some Bible scholars have pointed out that Genesis 2 (with Adam and Eve) and 2 Samuel 5 (with David and Israel) are the only two places in the Bible where the phrase "bone and flesh" are used in making a covenant. David is like a bridegroom king to Israel as his people-bride.

We see this idea again much later in David's life, during the time when his son Absalom briefly overthrows him and drives him out of Jerusalem. Absalom's evil general gives the traitorous son some vicious advice:

> "Let me choose twelve thousand men, and I will set out and pursue David tonight. . . . I will strike down the king only, and I will bring all the people back to you *as a bride comes home to her husband.*" (2 Sm 17:1–3)

The Covenant of David

So we can see that the image of husband and wife described the relationship of king to people. So, let's add the wedding ring to David's finger.

At this point, David looks a lot like Adam, which is not accidental. David was, in fact, a kind of new Adam figure, who marked a new beginning for humanity. Like Adam, he enjoyed the filial relationship with God and was king over much, if not all, of creation. David is also a type or image of Jesus Christ, who is called the "final Adam" by St. Paul (1 Cor 14:15).

David also resembles Israel—or what Israel should have become, if Israel had carefully followed the covenant given through Moses. God had said to Pharaoh, "Israel is my firstborn son" (Ex 4:22) and promised the people of Israel, "You shall be to me a *royal priesthood*" (Ex 19:6; emphasis mine). But these privileges were rejected at the golden calf, and during the nine rebellions in the desert in the Book of Numbers. The final form of the Mosaic Covenant, Deuteronomy, said very little about sonship, priesthood, or royalty for all Israel. So, what the nation as a whole was not able to claim, God now grants to David the King and his successors. Although the people of Israel may not enjoy the full rights of sonship, at least their king will—and the rest of the people can at least enjoy "trickle down" benefits.

In this way, the Davidic Covenant represents a step of progress in salvation history. Adam had divine sonship and lost it. It was offered again to Israel but rejected. Now Israel's king possesses it. If the people obey him, they will get at least indirect blessings of sonship. It's a step in the right direction toward a time when there will be a perfect Son of David who will also be the Son of God and will make divine sonship available for everyone.

So far, we've learned these five covenants:

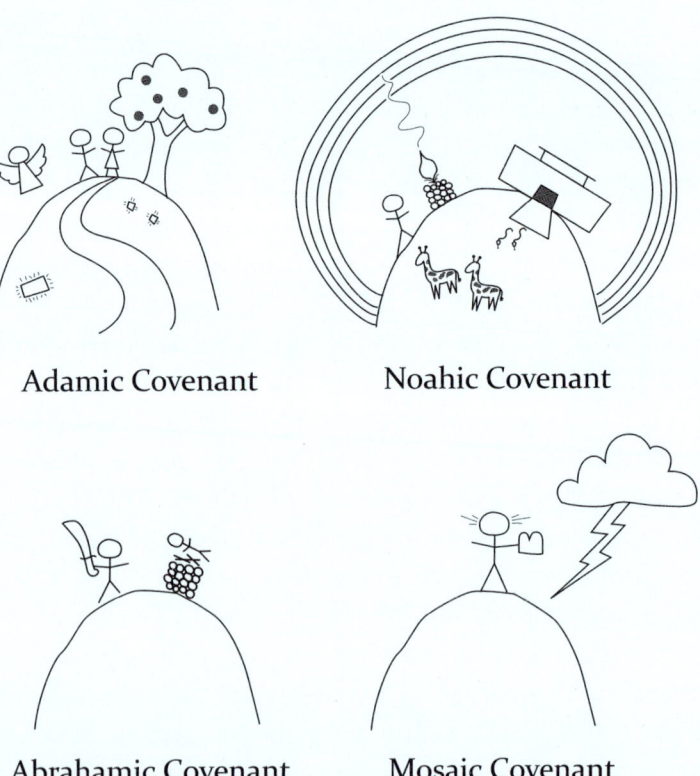

Adamic Covenant Noahic Covenant

Abrahamic Covenant Mosaic Covenant

The Covenant of David

Davidic Covenant

SELF-STUDY GUIDE

Background

This chapter explains that King David, not Moses, is the most important man in the Old Testament. After he is introduced in the Book of Ruth, his name appears more than one thousand times throughout the rest of the Old Testament. He is a king, and he is also a priest and a prophet. He was great in what he did for Israel as a historic nation (politics) and as a worshipping nation (liturgy), and for what he symbolized for the future of God's people (eschatology). David founded Jerusalem as the capital of Israel, and he brought the Ark of the Covenant to Jerusalem and gave it a permanent home. In the Davidic Covenant, God blessed David and his descendants with the blessings he once intended for Adam and the entire people of Israel before sin got in the way. From David's line, a messiah would come.

Text Reference (pages 106–109)

Exceptional in the areas of politics, liturgy, and eschatology, David's most serious weaknesses affected his personal life and domestic policies. His adulterous affair with Bathsheba, the wife of Uriah, who was one of his soldiers, is told in detail in 2 Samuel 11:1–12:25. David eventually plotted to have Uriah killed in battle and, after a period of mourning, married Bathsheba. She gave birth to a son who died soon after. Another son born to them, Solomon, eventually succeeded David as king. David admitted to his sins when confronted by the prophet Nathan. He repented, but his sins led

The Covenant of David

to difficult final years of his reign, including several family problems: a son raping his half sister; a revengeful murder by her brother; and a rebellious son, Absalom, who turned against his father. Eventually Absalom was killed by David's forces after becoming entangled in a tree, leading to great mourning by David: "O my son Ab'salom, O Ab'salom, my son, my son!" (2 Sm 19:4).

Reading Comprehension

1. Who were the judges?
2. Why did the people of Israel tire of being ruled by judges?
3. Explain the difference between the "Moses Channel" and the "David Channel."
4. Give one example for each category of David's greatness: political, liturgical, and eschatological.
5. Why was placing the capital of Israel in Jerusalem a shrewd political move for King David?
6. What was a key addition David added to worship besides moving the Ark to Jerusalem?
7. What does it mean to say that David was a "sign of one to come"?
8. What are three promises God makes to David about a son who will be David's heir?
9. How was David also a priest?
10. What is meant by the "trickle down" benefits for Israel on behalf of King David?

Reading in Context

In your notebook, match each of the terms used in this chapter with its definition below.

dominant   stability   eschatological   ultimate   elders

filial   strategic   scarcely   sanctuary

1. The best achievable or imaginable
2. A holy place or place of refuge
3. Firmness; steadiness
4. Referring to death, judgment, and final destiny
5. Most important, powerful, or influential
6. The generation or generations after the parental generation
7. Hardly; barely
8. Leaders or a senior figure in a group
9. Carefully designed to fulfill a particular purpose

Writing Assignment

David was not the only king to sin against God. Read and summarize in one sentence how each of the following kings of Israel sinned: Saul (1 Sm 15:1–9), Solomon (1 Kgs 11:1–10), Jeroboam (1 Kgs 14:1–10), Baasha (1 Kgs 16:1–6), Omri (1 Kgs 16:23–26), Joram (2 Kgs 3:1–3), Ahaziah (2 Kgs 8:25–27), Zechariah (2 Kgs 15:8–10), Ahaz (2 Kgs 16:1–4), Manesseh (2 Kgs 21:1–16), and Zedekiah (2 Kgs 14:18–25:7).

Small-Group Guide

Opening Prayer

Loving Father,

Thank you for this precious gift of your Word, through which we may come to know and worship you more fully and love you more deeply.

Lord Jesus Christ, today we gather as your disciples. We sit at your feet ready to listen to your Word. We humbly ask that you open our ears so that we may hear with our intellect and open our hearts so that we may know you intimately.

Come, Holy Spirit; fill us with your gifts of wisdom, understanding, and knowledge so that we may grow in love, faithfulness, and joy. Amen.

Discussion Questions

1. In the years following the Mosaic Covenant, the nation of Israel grows, but not without some growing pains. Nevertheless, it is in the Davidic Covenant that part of Abraham's blessings come to fruition.

   List David's characteristics. Connect them to Adam.

2. Describe how David fulfills Abraham's blessings and his role in salvation history.

3. David is described as "a great reformer who personally 'practiced what he preached'" (page 108).

Do you have an area in your spiritual life that could use a little reform? What small change could you implement in your practice of the faith that would refresh your relationship with the Lord or help you go deeper in your relationship?

4. Examine your faith life in relation to David's public displays of worship and praise. Are you ready to be as forthright in declaring your faith as he was?

   David wrote songs of worship. Perhaps writing praise music is not your cup of tea, but think about how you worship. Do you pray communal prayers in a strong and loud voice? Do you sing during Mass? Do you make the Sign of the Cross reverently and with confidence in public?

5. Consider how David is similar to Jesus Christ. Connect David to Jesus.

   How does God work through these covenants—the Adamic, Noahic, Abrahamic, Mosaic, and Davidic Covenants—to guide us as a people, align us to his will, and prepare us for the coming of his Son, Jesus Christ?

Bonus: In your notebook, draw a stick figure of yourself, joyful in your role as child of God. Add a symbol of your favorite psalm of thanksgiving, praise, or repentance.

Closing Prayer

Almighty Father,

Thank you for fulfilling your promises and for your grand design for your people. We are grateful for your paternal guidance and correction.

We praise you and glorify you in word and deed as we strive to grow and blossom as your sons and daughters. Bless us in our endeavor to live fully your teachings. Amen.

SIX
STORMY TODAY, SONNY TOMORROW
The New Covenant in the Prophets

Suggested Reading: 1 Kings 3-8

The Rise and Fall of the Davidic Covenant

The Davidic Covenant and kingdom did not reach their peak under David himself, but under his glorious son Solomon.

This is Solomon:

I always draw him with a really big crown. It's not just ridiculously big; it's ludicrously big. I put the ludicrous crown on Solomon because he was fabulously rich and also to distinguish him from David. The family resemblance is so strong, you wouldn't be able to tell them apart otherwise!

Solomon is remembered as the wisest man who ever lived. In the famous account in 1 Kings 3, Solomon was still quite young when his father David died and left him the kingdom. God appeared to him and offered to grant him whatever he asked for. Rather than requesting power, money, or long life, Solomon asked for wisdom to be a good ruler. God was pleased with this and granted him wisdom, along with the wealth and power he did not ask for.

For this reason, Solomon is the source and inspiration for the "Wisdom Literature" in the Bible: the Books of Proverbs, Ecclesiastes, Wisdom of Solomon, Song of Solomon, and Sirach. He didn't write all of those books personally, of course, but he started the tradition.

God's covenant with David had promised that his son would build the "house of God" or temple, and Solomon fulfilled this divine promise. In fact, the high point of the entire Old Testament comes in 1 Kings 8, when Solomon completes and dedicates his great temple to the LORD:

During the dedication ceremony, the priests and Levites bring the Ark of the Covenant and the other vessels and furnishings of Moses's Tabernacle into the Temple itself. This symbolized a transition: from now on, the Temple would take over from the Tabernacle built in the wilderness.

We have to pause a moment to ponder the Temple, in order to see that it was the symbol and sum of all the covenants and all salvation history. The Temple was decorated inside with pictures and engravings of flowers and animals, with plentiful gold and jewels in the Temple itself and its furnishings. The flowers, animals, gold, and jewels called to mind Eden and the Adamic Covenant. In fact, the stream that flowed out of the side of the temple mount was called "the Gihon" after one of the rivers that flowed from Eden (Gn 2:13; 1 Kgs 1:33).

The Temple was also a kind of "new ark." Just as Noah's ark was a "floating Eden," so scholars have pointed out intentional similarities in the way the Ark and the Temple were built. For example, both were constructed with three levels or decks (Gn 6:16; 1 Kgs 6:36).

The exact place where the Temple was built was highly significant: it was on the massive rock formation called "Moriah" or "Mount Moriah" (2 Chr 3:1) where Abraham had tried to sacrifice Isaac to God so many years before. In fact, as we mentioned earlier, later Jewish tradition holds that the animal sacrifices offered in the Temple were only pleasing to God because they reminded him of Isaac's self-offering on the same site so many years before. So the Temple has a strong relationship to the Abrahamic Covenant.

The Temple was also the successor of the Tabernacle of the Mosaic Covenant, symbolized especially by the transfer of the Ark inside the Temple. This act also symbolized the relationship between the two covenants. The Ark built by Moses moves inside the Temple built by Solomon. This means, in a sense, that the Davidic Covenant is absorbing (or *assimilating*) the Mosaic. From now on, the son of David, heir of David's covenant, will be responsible to make sure that Israel follows the Mosaic Covenant.

And, of course, the Temple itself is part of the very terms of the Davidic Covenant. The fact that it is standing at all, and that Solomon is there to pray to God and dedicate it to him (1 Kgs 8), is visible proof that God has kept the covenant promises given to David (2 Sm 7:12–13).

For the ancient Israelite worshiper, the importance of the Temple can hardly be overemphasized. The Temple was a standing reminder of the covenants with Adam, Noah, Abraham, Moses, and David. It summed up all salvation history and represented all God's relationships with his people. There was nothing greater than the Temple except God himself. Many years later, Jesus will describe his own presence by saying, "Something greater than the Temple is here" (Mt 12:6). When we understand how great the Temple was, we realize Jesus was claiming to be God.

So What Happened After Solomon?

First Kings 8, which describes the completion and dedication of Solomon's Temple, is the high point of the Old Testament. Everything else is downhill from there. Sadly, the decline starts during Solomon's own reign. Toward the end of his life, Solomon's foreign wives persuaded him to build shrines to their pagan gods, and Solomon was no longer dedicated to the LORD as he had once been (1 Kgs 11). He also began to tax the people of Israel harshly (1 Kgs 12:4).

After Solomon's reign was over, the northern ten tribes of Israel broke off from the House of David when Solomon's son Rehoboam refused to cut taxes (1 Kgs 12). They chose a different king, not from the line of David, and they returned to the worship of golden calves, like Israel in the desert.

The southern tribes of Judah and Benjamin stayed faithful to the son of David and to the Temple. The ten tribes in the north were called "the House of Israel," and the two tribes in the south were called "the House of Judah" (Jer 31:31). However, these two Israelite kingdoms were too weak to survive separately for very long. Both entered into a long period of decline. After about two hundred years, the northern kingdom of Israel was completely wiped out by the Assyrians, a huge foreign empire that controlled most of the Middle East at that time (2 Kgs 17). Most of the Israelite population (the northern ten tribes) was sent into exile to different places all over the known world and was never heard from again.

The southern kingdom of Judah held on for another 150 years or so before the Babylonians wiped it out in 587 BC and took most of the Jews as captives to Babylon (2 Kgs 25).

Prophets and Losses

So what was God doing with his people for these hundreds of years while the two Israelite kingdoms were losing power? He was sending them his prophets.

There are a lot of prophets in the Bible. We usually think of the four major prophets (Isaiah, Jeremiah, Ezekiel, and Daniel) and the twelve minor prophets (Hosea through Malachi). Most of these prophets did their prophesying while the kingdoms were in steep decline, although a few ministered during the exile (Ezekiel and Daniel) and some spoke God's word to the Jews who survived the exile and returned to Jerusalem (Haggai, Zechariah, and Malachi).

We're going to concentrate on the three great prophets of the Jewish tradition: Isaiah, Jeremiah, and Ezekiel. Each of these prophets, in their own way, are like weather men who see nothing but storms and gloom in the short-term outlook but whose "extended forecasts" are full of sunny days and pleasant temperatures. The "stormy weather" in the short term is due to the curses of the Mosaic Covenant, which the people are suffering because they've broken their covenant commitments (see Dt 28:15–68). The coming "sunny days"—or better, "Sonny days"—are the age when God will bring them a New Covenant: one without the Mosaic curses, one that will see the return of the Son of David, who will restore David's kingdom.

The New Covenant in Isaiah *(Isaiah 9:1-7, 11:1-6)*

The largest and best-loved of the prophetic books, the Book of Isaiah is sometimes called "the fifth gospel" because of its many prophecies of the Messiah and how often it is quoted in the New Testament.

Isaiah prophesied from about 740 BC to 700 BC. He does his share of criticizing the southern kingdom of Judah for being unfaithful to their covenant with God. He launches into harsh words almost from the start of his book:

> Ah, sinful nation, a people laden with iniquity, offspring of evildoers, sons who deal corruptly! They have forsaken the LORD, they have despised the Holy One of Israel, they are utterly estranged. (Is 1:4)

The New Covenant in the Prophets

He goes on like that for quite some time. However, it's not the negative words in Isaiah we want to look at. Instead, we want to focus on his hope for the future. Isaiah's hopes all swirl around the return of a really good Son of David who will be king over God's people. For example, in Isaiah 9 he says,

> But there will be no gloom for her that was in anguish. In the former time he brought into contempt the land of Zebulun and the land of Naphtali, but in the latter time he will make glorious the way of the sea, the land beyond the Jordan, Galilee of the nations. The people who walked in darkness have seen a great light; those who dwelt in a land of deep darkness, on them has light shined. For to us a child is born, to us a son is given; and the government will be upon his shoulder, and his name will be called "Wonderful Counselor, Mighty God, Everlasting Father, Prince of Peace." Of the increase of his government and of peace there will be no end, upon the throne of David, and over his kingdom, to establish it, and to uphold it with justice and with righteousness from this time forth and for evermore. (Is 9:1–2, 6–7)

Here, Isaiah is saying that the people in the north of Israel—the northern tribes of Zebulun and Naphtali, folks who had gotten the worst of it during the invasions that destroyed the two kingdoms—were going to be the first to see the birth of a new ruler, a Son of David who would be virtually divine ("Mighty God, Everlasting Father"). Though they've had stormy weather, they will one day bask in the "Sonshine" of David's heir.

A few chapters later, Isaiah again talks about this great king coming from the line of David:

> There shall come forth a shoot from the stump of Jesse, and a branch shall grow out of his roots.

> And the Spirit of the LORD shall rest upon him,
> the spirit of wisdom and understanding, the spirit
> of counsel and might, the spirit of knowledge and
> the fear of the LORD. And his delight shall be in the
> fear of the LORD. He shall not judge by what his
> eyes see, or decide by what his ears hear; but with
> righteousness he shall judge the poor, and decide
> with equity for the meek of the earth; and he shall
> smite the earth with the rod of his mouth, and
> with the breath of his lips he shall slay the wicked.
> Righteousness shall be the girdle of his waist, and
> faithfulness the girdle of his loins. (Is 11:1–5)

What does all that mean? Well, the "stump of Jesse" is what's left of the royal family, the family of David. Jesse was David's father. The "branch" that comes forth is a new royal Son. He's anointed with the Spirit of the Lord, which gives him every kind of wisdom. This reminds us of David, who was anointed with God's spirit. It also reminds us of Solomon, who had every kind of wisdom. So this new royal Son is going to be equal to or greater than David and Solomon (Mt 12:42). As a ruler, he's going to be especially kind to the poor and the meek.

Much later in the Book of Isaiah, the LORD actually speaks to this royal Son of David who is coming:

> I am the LORD, I have called you in righteousness,
> I have taken you by the hand and kept you; I have
> given you as a covenant to the people, a light to the
> nations. (Is 42:6)

Isaiah's words are striking because a person can't really be a covenant. One person can *make* a covenant with another, but a person can't *be* a covenant.

Even so, Isaiah records God saying to his Servant, who is probably the Son of David: "I have given you *as a covenant* to

The New Covenant in the Prophets

the people" (emphasis mine). So, we can say that Isaiah foresees a future in which there is going to be a New Covenant. This New Covenant is somehow going to be God's special Servant, who is the same person as the Son of David mentioned in Isaiah 9 and 11.

Let's look at one more passage in Isaiah, an astounding one that describes how this covenant is going to work and who is going to be a party to it:

> Ho, every one who thirsts, come to the waters; and he who has no money, come, buy and eat! Come, buy wine and milk without money and without price. Why do you spend your money for that which is not bread, and your labor for that which does not satisfy? Hearken diligently to me, and eat what is good, and delight yourselves in fatness. Incline your ear, and come to me; hear, that your soul may live; and I will make with you an everlasting covenant, my steadfast, sure love for David. (Is 55:1–3)

It's God speaking in these verses, and he's talking to poor people, people who are thirsty and hungry and have no money. He's inviting them to a meal; really, to a feast where they can "eat what is good and delight themselves in fatness." No Weight Watchers or calorie counting here! If these poor people will come to him and eat, he promises them a covenant: "I will make with you an everlasting *covenant*, my *steadfast, sure love* for David."

The Hebrew word for "covenant" is *berith*. Where the English has three words: "steadfast, sure love," the Hebrew has just one: *hesed*. It takes three English words to translate *hesed* because we just don't have a word like it in our language. *Hesed* has a very special meaning. It refers to *covenant love*, the kind of love that people in a covenant ought to show one another. It means *love, faithfulness, loyalty,* and *reliability*—all these things.

The "everlasting *berith*" that God offers to the poor people here is the same thing as "my *hesed* for David" or "my *covenant love* for David." In other words, the new, everlasting covenant is really going to be the *Davidic Covenant,* only now opened up to include anybody who will recognize that they are poor and need God. Any poor, hungry, thirsty person who comes and eats the meal God offers will enter into the Davidic Covenant. Hmmm, I think I see where this is all going. . . .

The New Covenant in Jeremiah *(Jeremiah 30-33)*

Jeremiah (about 645 BC–585 BC) has a reputation for usually being in a bad mood about what's not right in the world. His reputation may not be fair: after all, he just spoke and prophesied what God told him. Nonetheless, the majority of his book focuses on the failures of the people of Israel and Judah, and the consequences of their decision to turn away from the Lord and worship the idols of pagan gods:

> Be appalled, O heavens, at this, be shocked, be utterly desolate, says the Lord, for my people have committed two evils: they have forsaken me, the fountain of living waters, and dug out wells for themselves, broken wells, that can hold no water. (Jer 2:12–13)
>
> Surely, as a faithless wife leaves her husband, so have you been faithless to me, O house of Israel, says the Lord. (Jer 3:20)
>
> For the house of Israel and the house of Judah have been utterly faithless to me, says the Lord. They have spoken falsely of the Lord, and have said, "He will do nothing; no evil will come upon us, nor shall we see sword or famine." (Jer 5:11–12)

Because they have done this, the LORD is no longer going to protect them from their enemies. Instead, they will be on their own against the Babylonians, who are going to invade their land:

> Behold, I am bringing upon you a nation from afar, O house of Israel, says the LORD. . . . Their quiver is like an open tomb, they are all mighty men. They shall eat up your harvest and your food . . . your fortified cities in which you trust they shall destroy with the sword. (Jer 5:15–17)

That's Jeremiah's theme for most of the book.

However, there are four chapters where he is in a good mood: chapters 30–33. Scholars call these four chapters "the Book of Consolation" because it's where Jeremiah offers some hope to the people of Judah.

We want to look at some of the things Jeremiah says in the "Book of Consolation," starting right in the middle of the book, where Jeremiah makes the most famous prophecy of his entire career:

> Behold, the days are coming, says the LORD, when I will make a New Covenant with the house of Israel and the house of Judah, not like the covenant which I made with their fathers when I took them by the hand to bring them out of the land of Egypt, my covenant which they broke, and I showed myself their Master, says the LORD. But this is the covenant which I will make with the house of Israel after those days, says the LORD: I will put my law within them, and I will write it upon their hearts; and I will be their God, and they shall be my people. And no longer shall each man teach his neighbor and teach his brother, saying, "Know the LORD," for they shall all know me, from the least of them to the greatest, says the LORD; for I will

forgive their iniquity, and I will remember their sin no more. (Jer 31:31–34)

This is the only place in the Old Testament where the exact phrase "New Covenant" is used. When Jesus says, "This cup is the New Covenant in my blood" (Lk 22:20), he is making a direct connection with this prophecy of Jeremiah (Jer 31:31). Of course, we repeat these words at every Mass. Since every Mass is a fulfillment of what Jeremiah promised, it's worth our while to take a moment to try to understand what Jeremiah was promising.

Jeremiah contrasts this "New Covenant" with "the covenant which I made . . . when I took them out of Egypt." That is obviously the Mosaic Covenant. The New Covenant will not be like the Mosaic because the people of Israel broke the Mosaic—not only with the golden calf but also nine times in the wilderness. As we saw, the Mosaic Covenant had to be remade at least twice ("second Sinai" and Deuteronomy), and by the end, it was a patched-up affair that included some bad laws given just because the people's hearts were hard. They couldn't handle anything better.

Jeremiah is saying that, in the future, God is going to make a clean break with the old, patched-up Mosaic Covenant and just start over: the "New Covenant." How will this "New Covenant" be different than the old?

The old covenant was written on tablets of stone, first by God, and then (after the calf) by Moses. The New Covenant, however, will be "written on their hearts." Whatever the New Covenant is, it will be a matter of the inside, not the outside. It will mean an interior change for the people who enter it. This interior change will mean coming to know God—"they shall all know me"—and being forgiven of one's sin.

Elsewhere in the Book of Consolation, Jeremiah makes it clear that one day the covenant with David will be restored:

> Behold, the days are coming, says the LORD, when I will fulfill the promise I made to the house of Israel and the house of Judah. In those days and at that time I will cause a righteous Branch to spring forth for David; and he shall execute justice and righteousness in the land. (Jer 33:14–15)
>
> The word of the LORD came to Jeremiah: Thus says the LORD: If you can break my covenant with the day and my covenant with the night, so that day and night will not come at their appointed time, then also my covenant with David my servant may be broken, so that he shall not have a son to reign on his throne. (Jer 33:19–21)

So we notice a contrast. The "New Covenant" will not be like the Mosaic, which was broken. However, the Davidic Covenant is as unbreakable as the cycles of nature. It follows that the New Covenant will involve a restoration of the Davidic Covenant, in some way.

The New Covenant in Ezekiel *(Ezekiel 34, 36, 37)*

The last of the three great prophets of the Jewish tradition, Ezekiel sometimes reminds me of one of those "shock jock" radio personalities whose comments push the envelope for what you can get away with on the airwaves. His visual imagery is stunning and outlandish (Ez 1, 10), and some chapters of his book ought not to be read to children under seventeen (Ez 16, 23)! For these and other reasons, the rabbis almost didn't allow his book into the Jewish Bible, and even when they did accept it, they put restrictions on who could read it!

Ezekiel prophesied from about 590 to 570 BC, around the same time as Jeremiah, although he was a little younger than his fellow prophet. Jeremiah has the reputation for being the complaining prophet, but for most of his book, Ezekiel is scarcely more optimistic:

> Thus says the Lord God: This is Jerusalem; I have set her in the center of the nations, with countries round about her. And she has wickedly rebelled against my ordinances more than the nations, and against my statutes more than the countries round about her, by rejecting my ordinances and not walking in my statutes. Therefore thus says the Lord God . . . I will execute judgments in the midst of you in the sight of the nations. . . . "Thus shall my anger spend itself, and I will vent my fury upon them and satisfy myself; and they shall know that I, the Lord, have spoken in my jealousy, when I spend my fury upon them." (Ez 4:5–7, 5:13)

However, Ezekiel, like Jeremiah, has a sort of "Book of Consolation" in chapters 34–37, where he speaks of the good things to come after Israel and Judah are judged for breaking the old covenant. And, what's more, the Book of Ezekiel ends with a nine-chapter description of what the new Temple and the new Jerusalem will be like in the last times, when God restores the fortunes of his people (Ez 40–48).

For our purposes, we want to look in Ezekiel 34–37 to find prophesies about the "New Covenant" that are very similar to those in Jeremiah.

In Ezekiel 34, the prophet compares Israel to a flock of sheep. In the future, God promises to protect his sheep from their enemies:

> I will save my flock, they shall no longer be a prey; and I will judge between sheep and sheep. And I will set up over them one shepherd, my servant David, and he shall feed them: he shall feed them and be their shepherd. And I, the Lord, will be their God, and my servant David shall be prince

among them; I, the LORD, have spoken. (Ez 34:22–24)

Like Jeremiah, Ezekiel prophesies that "David"—which means the Davidic king, a descendant of David—will be restored as king of Israel in the future. This would involve a restoration of the Davidic Covenant.

Ezekiel continues his prophecy:

> I will make with them a *covenant of peace* and banish wild beasts from the land, so that they may dwell securely in the wilderness and sleep in the woods. And I will make them and the places round about my hill a blessing; and I will send down the showers in their season; they shall be showers of blessing. (Ez 34:25–26; emphasis mine)

What Jeremiah calls the "New Covenant," Ezekiel calls the "covenant of peace." The name "covenant of peace" (*shalom*) calls to mind the peaceful covenant that existed between God, humans, and creation in Eden. We can see the Eden imagery in the lines above. In this new "covenant of peace," dangerous beasts will be no more, and people will be able to sleep in the forests. Gentle rains will fall, making the countryside fertile. In short, everything will be like Eden.

Ezekiel continues to describe the situation in the latter times in chapter 36:

> For I will take you from the nations, and gather you from all the countries, and bring you into your own land. I will sprinkle clean water upon you, and you shall be clean from all your uncleannesses, and from all your idols I will cleanse you. A new heart I will give you, and a new spirit I will put within you; and I will take out of your flesh the heart of stone and give you a heart of flesh. And I will put my spirit within you, and cause you to walk in my

statutes and be careful to observe my ordinances. (Ez 36:24–27)

Here there is much in common with Jeremiah's description of the "New Covenant." Jeremiah spoke of God writing the New Covenant on the heart; Ezekiel uses a similar image, speaking of God giving Israel a "new heart and a new Spirit" so they will be able to follow God's law. This gift of a "new Spirit" will follow a "sprinkling with clean water," which will cleanse God's people from their sins.

As we move into the next chapter, we find out that resurrection will also be part of the new situation in the latter days:

> Therefore prophesy, and say to them, Thus says the LORD GOD: Behold, I will open your graves, and raise you from your graves, O my people; and I will bring you home into the land of Israel. And you shall know that I am the LORD, when I open your graves, and raise you from your graves, O my people. And I will put my Spirit within you, and you shall live. (Ez 37:12–14)

Here again, we have the promise of God putting his Spirit in his people. Finally, Ezekiel summarizes the situation of the "covenant of peace":

> My servant David shall be king over them; and they shall all have one shepherd. They shall follow my ordinances and be careful to observe my statutes. . . . I will make a *covenant of peace* with them; it shall be an *eternal covenant* with them; and I will bless them and multiply them, and will set my sanctuary in the midst of them for evermore. My dwelling place shall be with them; and I will be their God, and they shall be my people. (Ez 37:24–27; emphasis mine)

The New Covenant in the Prophets

Again, the promise of the return of the Davidic king is given, implying that the Davidic Covenant will be restored. Then Ezekiel adds the name "everlasting covenant" to the covenant of peace. In the Mass, the Church combines Jeremiah's phrase "New Covenant" with Ezekiel's phrase "everlasting covenant" and says, "the new and everlasting covenant," or "the new and eternal covenant," which means the same. Ezekiel also mentions something very significant about this new, everlasting covenant: it will involve God setting his sanctuary in the midst of his people—in other words, a new temple to replace the old one that was destroyed by the Babylonians. The promise of a new temple can also be found in Isaiah and Jeremiah, although we don't have time to look at those prophecies. The new temple is very important to Ezekiel, who was a priest and spent a lot of his time in the old temple. In fact, as I mentioned above, the last nine chapters of his book are largely a description of this new temple.

To recap, the great prophets criticized the people for breaking the Old Covenant but comforted the people with the promise of a New Covenant. This New Covenant would be granted on a new or renewed Mount Zion. So we're going to put our prophet on the new Zion. "Zion" is drawn with dotted lines because it's a future reality. The "new Zion" or "new Jerusalem" is expected but hasn't arrived yet:

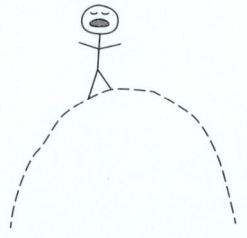

Now, as we've seen, this New Covenant spoken of by the prophets includes the restoration and transformation of the Davidic Covenant. The Davidic king is going to return, so let's put him in with dotted lines:

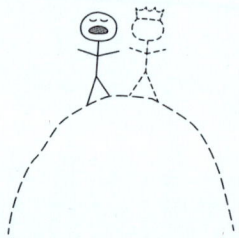

And, as Ezekiel especially emphasizes, we are going to get a new temple as well:

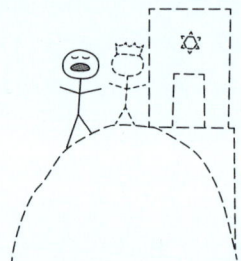

There. That's our icon for the New Covenant in the prophets. This is how far we've come in salvation history:

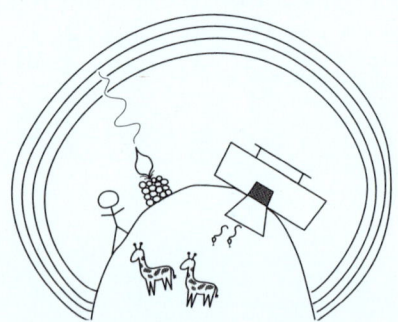

Adamic Covenant   Noahic Covenant

The New Covenant in the Prophets

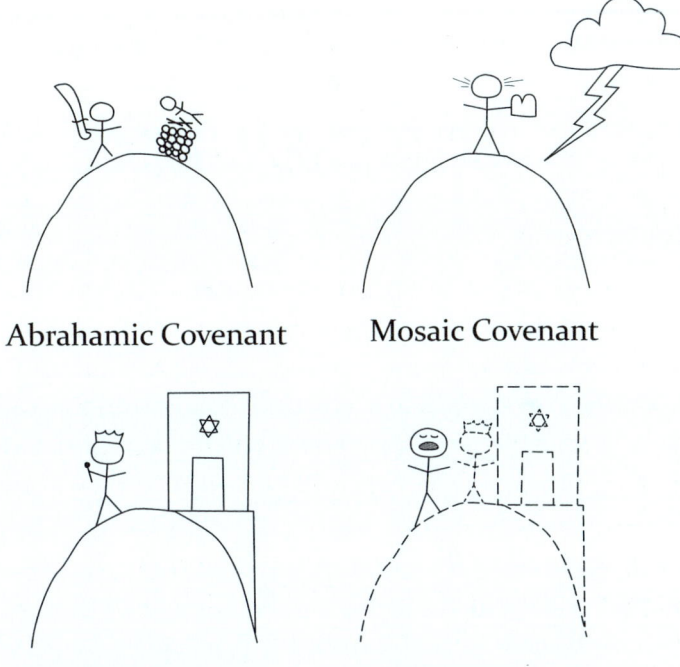

SELF-STUDY GUIDE

Background

The covenants of the prophets connect backward with the previous Old Testament covenants and also look forward "in expectation of a new and everlasting Covenant for all, to be written on their hearts" (Heb 10:16, quoted in *CCC*, 64; cf. Is 1:2–4 and Jer 31:31–34). Through the prophets God readied Israel to accept salvation that would come through Jesus Christ, the Son of God, and be opened to all of humanity. The prophets Isaiah, Ezekiel, and Jeremiah—featured in this chapter—present dire warnings for their current day coupled with good news for the long term with the hope of a new King David.

Reading Comprehension

1. List ways that Solomon's Temple symbolized and summed up all of the covenants and all of salvation history to that point.

2. If the completion and dedication of Solomon's Temple was the high point of the Old Testament, how did things decline right away afterward?

3. Explain the reasons for the division of the ten northern tribes and the southern tribes of Judah and Benjamin.

4. What is meant by the "stump of Jesse" in the Book of Isaiah?

5. According to Isaiah, how will his covenant with God work, and who will be a part of it?

The New Covenant in the Prophets

6. What is Jeremiah's theme for most of the Book of Jeremiah?
7. Where is Jeremiah's New Covenant written (in comparison with the Mosaic Covenant)?
8. What does Ezekiel compare Israel to?
9. What does Ezekiel's "covenant of peace" call to mind?
10. What do Jeremiah's covenant and Ezekiel's covenant have in common?

Reading in Context

All of the following sentences are false. In your notebook, replace the italicized word with a word from this chapter to make the sentences true.

1. The Temple in Jerusalem was built on *Mount Sinai* where Abraham had tried to sacrifice Isaac years ago.
2. *King David* is the source and inspiration for the Wisdom Literature.
3. The ten tribes of the northern kingdom were completely wiped out by the *Babylonians*, an empire that controlled most of the Middle East.
4. There are four major prophets commonly known in the Bible: Isaiah, Jeremiah, Ezekiel, and *Hosea*.
5. The "everlasting berith" refers to the *Adamic* Covenant.
6. The only place in the Old Testament where the term "New Covenant" is known is in the Book of *Isaiah*.
7. Rather than referring to the "New Covenant," Ezekiel calls it a "covenant of *hope*."
8. Ezekiel emphasizes that God's people will get a new *Ark of the Covenant*.

Writing and Drawing Assignment

Browse the Books of Isaiah, Jeremiah, and Ezekiel and draw a sketch representing each prophet, his actions, or his words. Label the passages you are illustrating and write captions explaining the sketches.

Suggestions

- Isaiah: the Song of the Vineyard (5:1–7); hope for the Son of David (9:1–2, 6–7); "There shall come forth a shoot from the stump of Jesse" (11:1)
- Jeremiah: the prophet wearing thongs and a yoke on his shoulders (13:1–4, 27:2); the broken wine flask (13:12–14); the potter's vessel (18:1–12)
- Ezekiel: the four winged creatures (1:10–14); parable of the shepherds (34); vision of dry bones (37:1–14)

Small-Group Guide

Opening Prayer

Loving Father,

Thank you for this precious gift of your Word, through which we may come to know and worship you more fully and love you more deeply.

Lord Jesus Christ, today we gather as your disciples. We sit at your feet ready to listen to your Word. We humbly ask that you open our ears so that we may hear with our intellect and open our hearts so that we may know you intimately.

Come, Holy Spirit; fill us with your gifts of wisdom, understanding, and knowledge so that we may grow in love, faithfulness, and joy. Amen.

Discussion Questions

1. The period of the prophets marks a transition for the Jewish people. The Davidic Covenant has fallen apart, and the Jewish nation is fragmented and spreading further away from Jerusalem. Some have outright rejected God and returned to pagan worship. It is a time marked by exile, captivity, and even annihilation of some tribes of Israel. God sees this and repeatedly sends prophets to warn his people of the error of their ways.

   Name the three primary prophets and briefly explain their contribution to the New Covenant. What were their warnings?

What promises about the New Covenant are inherent in each of the three primary prophets' teachings? How do these promises affect your faith today?

2. Describe, in your own words, Israel's decline during this period of time. Include a discussion about Israel's political identity and how that may have affected the Israelites' identity as God's people. How might this also affect them personally in their relationship with the Lord?

   Explain how God continued to support the Israelites in spite of their quarreling and their departure from David's and Solomon's earlier examples.

3. What have you learned about God's commitment to his people during this period of the prophets?

   Have you ever experienced a period of doubt or felt yourself drifting away from the faith? What brought you back? Did you feel or see evidence of God's presence in your life during a dark time?

4. Examine the New Covenant in relation to "God setting his sanctuary in the midst of his people" (page 141). Explain how "sanctuary" is used here.

   What does the creation of a new Temple mean for the Jewish people? And what does it mean for us as Christians today?

5. The prophets were strong personalities, but they were charged by God to deliver a strong message. How were they received? Were their warnings heeded?

   Do you have a favorite prophet, or are you drawn in a particular way to a prophet because of certain characteristics? Why?

How do you respond to people today who carry God's message in the media or social media?

Bonus: In your notebook, draw a stick figure of yourself, joyful in your role as child of God. Add a symbol of a gift you would ask of God.

Closing Prayer

Generous Father,

Thank you for fulfilling your promises and for your concern and watchfulness over our lives, especially when we wander away from your path. We are grateful for your paternal guidance and correction.

We praise you and glorify you in word and deed as we strive to recommit ourselves to you.

Bless us in our endeavor to live fully your teachings. Amen.

SEVEN
THE GRAND FINALE
The Eucharistic Covenant

Suggested Reading: Luke 22-24; Acts 1-2

Ezekiel, the last of the three great prophets of the Jewish tradition, finished prophesying around 570 BC. That means it was about 570 years before Jesus appeared in history. What was going on in the meantime?

The prophet Daniel was only a little younger than Ezekiel and prophesied shortly after him. Roughly thirty years after the death of Ezekiel, Daniel received a vision from God that it would take about five hundred years ("seventy weeks of years") for all the prophecies to be fulfilled (Dn 9:24–27). And so it did.

Of course, a lot happened in that time. In 539 BC, about the time Daniel was having his vision, the Persians conquered the Babylonians and took over the Middle East. The Persians were nicer than the Babylonians and let all the captured peoples go home, including the Jews. This is what we call "the return from exile."

Led by the prince Zerubbabel, the prophet Ezra, the aristocrat Nehemiah, and many other prophets and noblemen, the

Jews came back from Babylon in several waves in the late 500s and early 400s. By 515 BC, they had built another temple on the site of the old one, but it was a pretty sorry shack compared to the magnificent building Solomon had put up. But at least they had a place to worship God once again.

The return from exile was a mixed bag. On the positive side, the Jews had much of their land back, and they had a temple to worship God. On the other hand, they didn't have a Davidic king on the throne, their temple was a disappointment, and there was no sign of the New Covenant and the glorious New Temple that the prophets had promised. In fact, the Jews weren't even able to rule themselves. At first they were under the power of the Persians, and then after Alexander the Great swept through the Middle East in the 330s, they were ruled by him and his Greek-speaking successors (1 Mc 1:1–8).

However, two events gave rise to false hopes that the predictions of the great prophets were about to be fulfilled.

In the 160s BC, one of Alexander's successors, King Antiochus IV, whose capital was in Syria, took a hard line against the Jews he ruled. He tried to make them give up their religion. The Jews revolted under the leadership of a family of Levites known as the Maccabees (known also as the Hasmoneans). The Maccabees fought a guerilla war against the armies of Antiochus and eventually drove them out of Israel (1 Mc). For the next hundred years, the Maccabees ruled as kings, and they expanded the kingdom of Israel almost to the boundaries it had under David and Solomon.

Things were looking pretty good for the Jews at that point. They had their kingdom and most of their land back. Their temple was up and running. Once again, they were prosperous. There was just one problem: their kings had the wrong genealogy. They were Levites, not sons of David. They weren't supposed to be ruling. There was no way they could fulfill the prophecies. Their power ended in 63 BC when the Romans captured Jerusalem and divided the land of Israel into several provinces.

Shortly after the Maccabees, the hopes of the Jews were raised once again. When the Maccabean dynasty was declining and losing its grip on the land of Israel, a certain Herod, a nobleman from the south, went to Rome and had himself appointed king of Israel by the Romans. With the help of the Roman army, he gained control of the Jews without much difficulty and reigned quite successfully for about thirty years (about 37 BC–4 BC). Once again he extended the borders of Israel almost to the size of the kingdom under David and Solomon. What's more, he began to rebuild the temple on a massive scale, a temple even more impressive than Solomon's temple of old.

Again, things seemed to be going well for the Jewish nation. They had their kingdom back, more or less. They were building a new temple. They were prosperous. There was only one problem: Herod had the wrong genealogy, too. He wasn't a son of David any more than the Maccabees. He wasn't even a true Jew. He was a descendant of Esau, Jacob's hairy twin brother (Gn 25:25). There was no way that Herod or his successors could be the fulfillment of all the prophecies. Their rule effectively ended in AD 66, and the last of the Herods died in AD 92.

So we see that, in the time between the last of the prophets and the birth of Jesus, there had been some high points in Jewish history when all the signs were favorable and it looked as though the prophecies might soon be fulfilled. In each case, however, there was a nagging difficulty: the ruling family was from the wrong bloodline. For the prophecies to come true, they needed a descendant of David who could restore the Davidic Covenant. Now maybe we can better understand why the New Testament begins with these words: "The book of the genealogy of Jesus Christ, the *son of David*, the son of Abraham" (emphasis mine). For most modern Americans, genealogies are boring. But if you are a Jew in ancient times, and you've been waiting around for hundreds of years for a man with the right bloodline, *this* genealogy is anything but boring!

Jesus and the Covenants

Let's look more closely at how St. Matthew chooses to begin his biography of Jesus, which we call "The Gospel according to Matthew":

> This is the genealogy of Jesus the Christ, the son of David, the son of Abraham. (Mt 1:1)

Notice that Matthew does not call Jesus "*a* son of David" or "*a* son of Abraham." There were many sons of Abraham around—every Jew was a son of Abraham. There were other descendants of David around, too—some of them are mentioned by the ancient historians.

But Jesus wasn't just *any* descendant of David and Abraham. He was *the* son of David, *the* son of Abraham. In other words, he was *the promised* son of David and Abraham, *the* son who would fulfill all the promises of these two great covenants! By calling Jesus "*the* son of David, *the* son of Abraham," Matthew is talking about covenant fulfillment. Although in this verse Matthew mentions only David and Abraham, in fact Jesus fulfills all the expectations associated with each of the great covenants we have looked at in the Old Testament. Let's take a moment to walk through each of these covenants and see how Jesus fulfills their expectations.

Jesus and the Adamic Covenant

Adam was the father of the human race who held a fivefold role as son of God, king, priest, prophet, and bridegroom. Jesus is the "father" of a new race of humans, and if we read the gospels carefully, we see repeated signs that Jesus holds all five Adamic roles.

It's clear from the beginning of Matthew that Jesus is the Son of God. Although he is the legal son of St. Joseph (Mt 1:1–16), he is the actual Son of God through the power of the Holy Spirit. That's the point of the virgin birth (Mt 1:18–25). God the Father confirms Jesus's sonship also at his baptism, when he speaks in an audible voice from heaven: "This is my beloved son, in whom I am well pleased" (Mt 3:17):

(I'm sure the Lord will forgive us for these simple stick figures! He also used humble examples as a way to teach!)

God the Father repeats almost the same words at Jesus's Transfiguration (Mt 17:5). Because of his special sonship, Jesus calls God his Father, especially while praying (Mt 6:9; 11:25–27). Jesus even calls God his "Abba" (Mk 14:6), a word for "father" used by Jewish children, an intimate name perhaps close to our "papa."

Of course, it is clear that Jesus is the King, the Son of David. Both Matthew and Luke provide Jesus's genealogy going back to David (Mt 1:1–17; Lk 3:23–38). The angel Gabriel tells the Blessed Virgin Mary before his birth, "The Lord God will give to him the throne of his father David and he will reign over the house of Jacob forever" (Lk 1:32–33). During his lifetime, many people recognized his royalty, calling him "Son of David," especially after he performed miracles like exorcisms (Mt 12:23; 15:22). Nearing the time of his suffering and death, Jesus rode into Jerusalem on a donkey, intentionally imitating the great Solomon of old (Mt 21:2–7; see 1 Kgs 1:38–40). Ironically, even the Roman governor Pilate officially recognizes Jesus as the "King of the Jews" and has that title posted above Jesus on the cross (Jn 19:19–22).

Jesus's role as priest is harder to see, but it is there. For example, when the Pharisees challenge Jesus for breaking their Sabbath rules about rest, Jesus says, "Have you not read in the Law how on the Sabbath the priests in the Temple

The Eucharistic Covenant

profane the Sabbath, and are guiltless?" (Mt 12:5). Jesus points out that priests are allowed to work on the holy days; in fact, they have to. The implication is that Jesus himself is a priest and has priestly rights. Later, at his crucifixion, the apostle John mentions that Jesus's tunic "was without seam, woven from top to bottom" (John 19:23). What's the point of this insignificant little detail? Why even mention it? It's because in ancient times, the robe of the High Priest was woven without seams. Jesus's garment was a sign of his high priestly role. The Letter to the Hebrews discusses this role in great depth—in fact, one could argue that it is the main theme of the letter (see Heb 4:14–5:10; 7:1–10:18).

No one doubted that Jesus was also a prophet. When Jesus asks his disciples, "Who do people say that I am?" the disciples provide a list of various prophets: "Some say John the Baptist, others say Elijah, and others Jeremiah or one of the prophets" (Mt 16:13–15). Jesus calls himself a prophet. When he is scorned by the people in his own hometown, he says, "A prophet is not without honor except in his own country and in his own house" (Mt 13:57). When Jesus finally rides into

Jerusalem on Palm Sunday, the crowds announce, "This is the prophet Jesus from Nazareth in Galilee" (Mt 21:11).

Finally, Jesus was and is the Bridegroom. When questioned about Jesus, John the Baptist explained, "You yourselves bear me witness, that I said, I am not the Christ, but I have been sent before him. He who has the bride is the bridegroom; the friend of the bridegroom, who stands and hears him, rejoices greatly at the bridegroom's voice; therefore this joy of mine is now full. He must increase, but I must decrease" (Jn 3:28–30). Jesus himself suggests he is the "Bridegroom" when he tells parables about the kingdom that are based on wedding images: "The kingdom of heaven may be compared to a king who gave a marriage feast for his son" (Mt 22:2) or, "The kingdom of heaven shall be compared to ten virgins who took their lamps and went to meet the Bridegroom" (Mt 25:1). Jesus is the New Bridegroom, who offers himself in marriage to all humanity. To be "married" to Christ is to become part of the Church, his bride.

Son of God, king, priest, prophet, and bridegroom: Jesus fulfills all the roles of Adam. With Jesus, we begin a new chapter in the history of humanity. In fact, it is more than a new chapter: it is an entirely new beginning, a new creation. For that reason, St. Paul says, "If anyone is in Christ, he is a new creation!" (2 Cor 5:17). Likewise, St. John begins his gospel with the words "In the beginning was the Word," which are an imitation of the opening line of Genesis: "In the beginning God created." St. John's point is that Jesus marks such a radical turning point in human history, it is like the whole world has just started all over. Actually, St. Matthew makes almost the exact same point as St. John in the very first verse of the New Testament, although the point is made quietly so it's easy to miss. St. Matthew begins, "The book of the genealogy of Jesus Christ." The phrase "book of the genealogy of" occurs in only one other verse in the Bible, Genesis 5:1: "This is the book of the genealogy of Adam." St. Matthew is suggesting the same thing as St. John: Jesus is like a new Adam, and the Gospel is a new beginning and a new Genesis.

Now that we've laid the foundation of Jesus's relationship to the Adamic Covenant, we can move more quickly through the remaining covenants.

The Noahic Covenant

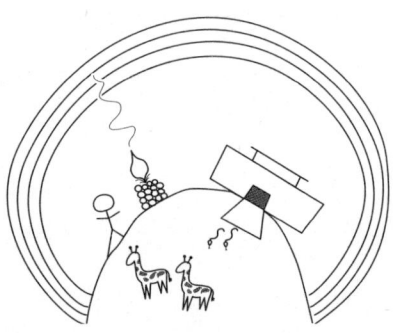

There is not much to say here, since the Gospel authors do not spend much time on the relationship between Jesus and Noah. But Noah himself was primarily a new Adam character, a second father to the whole human race. So all Jesus's Adamic characteristics also serve to connect him to Noah, who himself was a second Adam.

The Abrahamic Covenant

St. Matthew begins his gospel by calling Jesus "the son of David, the son of Abraham," which points out the importance of these two covenants, the Davidic and Abrahamic, in his understanding of Jesus.

Abraham's heir and only son by his first and legitimate wife Sarah was Isaac. Calling Jesus "*the* Son of Abraham" sets up a comparison between Jesus and Abraham's son Isaac. The parallel is strong, especially when we think of the most important event in Abraham and Isaac's life: the near-sacrifice on Mount Moriah. We have already discussed how this was a "mime" of Calvary: the one-and-only son carries the wood of his sacrifice up the mountain, where he is laid on the wood and offered to God out of love for his father. We have already discussed how the covenant with Abraham is finalized by God after the sacrifice of Isaac:

> And the angel of the LORD called to Abraham a second time from heaven, and said, "By myself I have sworn, says the LORD, because you have done this, and have not withheld your son, your only begotten son, I will indeed bless you . . . and *by your seed shall all the nations of the earth be blessed*, because you have obeyed my voice." (Gn 22:15–18; emphasis mine)

As I mentioned earlier, *seed* can be singular or plural. Jesus is the one promised "seed of Abraham" through whom blessing is going to come to all the nations of the earth. Only he can fulfill the entire promise of the covenant with Abraham.

The Mosaic Covenant

As we saw, the Mosaic Covenant got messed up pretty badly during the wilderness wanderings—there were at least nine different rebellions—so that by the end of Deuteronomy it's like a beat-up Ford sedan, blowing blue smoke out of the tailpipe and one wheel hanging on by a single lug nut.

Jesus comes as the great mechanic.

One of Moses's last promises was that a great prophet like himself would come some day: "The LORD your God will raise up for you a prophet like me from among you, from your brethren: you must listen to him!" (Dt 18:15). Now, "like" can mean either "similar to" or "equal to." In one sense, Moses's words applied to all the prophets because all the prophets were "similar to" Moses in various ways. However, none of the later prophets were *equal to* Moses. The last words of Deuteronomy stress, "And there has not arisen a prophet since in Israel like Moses, whom the LORD knew face to face" (Dt 34:10).

But the Gospel of John asserts Jesus is not only *equal* but also *superior* to Moses. Examine this verse from the opening of the Gospel of John:

> For the law was given through Moses; grace and truth came through Jesus Christ. No one has ever seen God; the only Son, who is in the bosom of the Father, he has made him known. (Jn 1:17–18)

Let's work through John 1:17–18 phrase by phrase: "For the law was given through Moses."

The Law. Yay.

Yay. One cheer for that.
"Grace and truth came through Jesus Christ!"

Grace + Truth!
Hip, hip, hooray!

Yes! Hip, hip, hooray! Hip, hip, *hooray! Hip,* hip, hooray!
"No one has ever seen God." This is a not-so-subtle remark about Moses, reminding us that, although he was the greatest prophet ever, he only saw God's back (Ex 33:18–23).

"The only Son, who is in the bosom of the Father, he has made him known." Not only has Jesus seen God, but Jesus *shows us* God. When you look at Jesus, you behold the face of God. As Jesus says to Philip at the Last Supper, "He who has seen me, has seen the Father" (Jn 14:9).

Jesus comes as a prophet *like* Moses but even greater than Moses.

Like Moses, Jesus goes up on a mountaintop in order to teach people God's law (Mt 5–7). But Jesus goes beyond Moses and even corrects defects Moses had allowed into the Law. For example, Moses permitted divorce because of the "hardness of heart" of the Israelite men (Dt 24:1; Mt 19:8). Jesus restores marriage to God's original plan of permanence (Mt 5:31–32). Moses permitted—even, in a sense, commanded—hatred for enemies (Dt 20:16–18), but Jesus corrects that with a universal command of love (Mt 5:44–45).

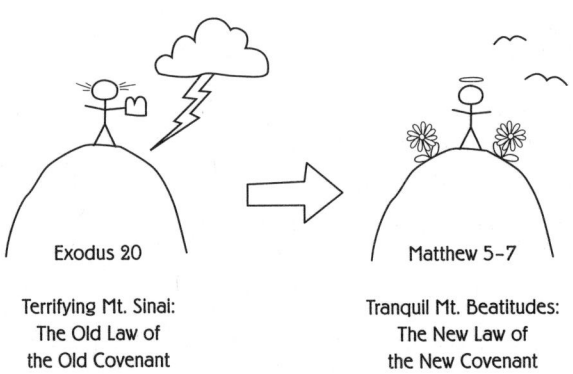

Exodus 20
Terrifying Mt. Sinai:
The Old Law of
the Old Covenant

Matthew 5–7
Tranquil Mt. Beatitudes:
The New Law of
the New Covenant

Like Moses, Jesus provides the people with supernatural bread, "bread from heaven" (Ex 16:1–36; Jn 6:1–14). When the people witness Jesus multiplying the loaves, they say, "This is indeed *the prophet* who is to come into the world!" (Jn 6:14, emphasis mine). What they mean by "the prophet" is "the prophet like Moses" of Deuteronomy 18:15. However, unlike the manna in the wilderness, the bread of Jesus leads to eternal life (Jn 6:51–58).

Like Moses, Jesus establishes a Passover for the people of God (Ex 12–13; Lk 22:7–30). But the sacrifice of Moses's Passover was just a sheep, and the blood of animals cannot take away sin (Ps 50:13; Heb 10:4). The sacrifice of Jesus's Passover is his very self, and his blood permanently washes us of sin (Jn 1:29; Heb 9:12; Rv 7:14).

We could write a whole book comparing Moses and Jesus: in fact, several have been written. However, let's sum it up like this: Moses was replaced by *Y'shua* (a.k.a. Joshua) who did what Moses failed to do: he led the people into the Promised Land. Now, in the New Testament, there comes another *Y'shua* (a.k.a. Jesus) who does what Moses and his covenant could not do: bring God's people into the Promised Land of heaven.

The Davidic Covenant

Above, when discussing Jesus as King as part of his fulfillment of the fivefold role of Adam, we already observed many of the ways in which the gospels point to Jesus as the Son of David who fulfills the covenant of  David. The main statement of the Davidic Covenant in the Old Testament is in 2 Samuel 7. Let's quote the heart of it once more:

> When your days are fulfilled and you lie down with your fathers, I will raise up your seed after you, who shall come forth from your body, and I will establish his kingdom. He shall build a house for my name, and I will establish the throne of his kingdom for ever. I will be his father, and he shall

> be my son.... And your house and your kingdom shall be made sure for ever before me; your throne shall be established for ever. (2 Sm 7:12–14)

The basic promises of this covenant can be listed as follows: (1) David will have a son and heir; (2) this son will build the Temple of God; (3) this son will also be the Son of God, and (4) this son will rule over the kingdom of David forever. Solomon, of course, was an initial fulfillment of these promises. He was David's own son and heir; he did build a stone temple for God; he was adopted as Son of God according to the covenant; and, he ruled for a long time. That's a close, but not perfect, fulfillment of the promises of the covenant.

When Jesus arrives in the gospels, we begin to realize that "one greater than Solomon is here" (Mt 12:42). The two genealogies of Jesus (in Matthew 1 and Luke 3) emphasize Jesus as David's true son. A traditional way of understanding the two different genealogies is that one shows Jesus's *legal lineage* and the other shows Jesus's *biological lineage*. Jesus is not only a true biological son of David (through Mary) but also the one with the right to claim the throne: he is both *son* and *heir*. At the same time, both Matthew and Luke insist that the conception of Christ was the result of the Holy Spirit, so that Jesus is the true Son of God, and not just by adoption. As the covenant with David said, "He will be my son, and I will be his father" (2 Sm 7:14).

Solomon built a house of stone for the worship of God. But that temple was torn down and no longer exists. Moreover, God doesn't really live in stone buildings. So there is a need for a better temple. When Jesus drives the moneychangers out of Herod's temple in the Gospel of John, the Jews are offended:

> The Jews then said to him, "What sign have you to show us for doing this?" Jesus answered them, "Destroy this temple, and in three days I will raise it up." The Jews then said, "It has taken forty-six years to build this temple, and will you raise it up in three days?" *But he spoke of the temple of his body.* (Jn 2:18–21; emphasis mine)

Jesus gives us a better temple than Solomon: a living temple, the temple of his body. Since a temple is where God dwells, this means, first of all, that God's presence dwells in Jesus's own body. However, since Jesus gives us his body to eat in the Eucharist, and since everyone knows that "you are what you eat," we too become the temple of God. So the Church is also a temple. This is a temple that cannot be torn down and will never pass away. It is as superior to the old temple as a human being is superior to lifeless stone.

Even when they tried to destroy the new temple—that is, Jesus's body—God wouldn't let it happen. He "raised up" Jesus from the grave—and the Church Fathers rightly saw this as a fulfillment of the promise to David that God would "raise up" David's seed after him (2 Sm 7:12). And once raised up, Jesus ascended to the right hand of God, where he rules over the kingdom literally *forever.* Solomon ruled a long time, but a long time is not forever. Only Jesus literally fulfills what was promised to David: "I will establish the throne of his kingdom *forever.*" The prophecy of Jeremiah is also fulfilled: "David shall never lack a man to sit on the throne of Israel" (Jer 33:17).

The New Covenant Promised by the Prophets

As we saw, the promised New Covenant did involve the fulfillment of the Davidic Covenant as part of its whole arrangement. But the New Covenant

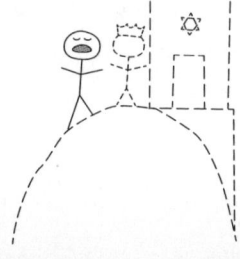

involved more than that. Isaiah foresaw God's special servant actually *becoming* a covenant. Jeremiah spoke of the law being written on people's hearts, and Ezekiel predicted a new Spirit being poured out on God's people.

Let's take a look at the most important passage for understanding how Jesus inaugurated the New Covenant, a part of Luke called the "Institution Narrative," because it *narrates* the *institution* (or *establishment*) of the Eucharist:

> Then came the day of Unleavened Bread, on which the passover lamb had to be sacrificed. So Jesus sent Peter and John, saying, "Go and prepare the passover for us, that we may eat it." . . . (Lk 22:7–8)
>
> And when the hour came, he sat at table, and the apostles with him. And he said to them, "I have earnestly desired to eat this passover with you before I suffer; for I tell you I shall not eat it until it is fulfilled in the kingdom of God." And he took a cup, and when he had given thanks he said, "Take this, and divide it among yourselves; for I tell you that from now on I shall not drink of the fruit of the vine until the kingdom of God comes." And he took bread, and when he had given thanks he broke it and gave it to them, saying, "This is my body which is given for you. Do this in remembrance of me." And likewise the cup after supper, saying, "This cup which is poured out for you is *the new covenant in my blood.*" (Lk 22:14–20; emphasis mine)

This is one of the most important events in human history. We are moving from the Old Covenant (Mosaic) to the New Covenant. There are two major connections to the Old Covenant: First, it's Passover time, and Jesus is celebrating the Passover. The Passover was, in many ways, the biggest holiday and the main sacrifice of the Old Covenant. Second, Jesus refers to the sacrifices at Sinai when Moses confirmed the Old

Covenant with the people of Israel. At the foot of Sinai, Moses sprinkled the blood of the lambs on God's altar and on the people, saying, "Look! The blood of the covenant!" (Ex 24:8). Jesus says something similar, "This cup is the new covenant in my blood." Once more, it's the *blood of the covenant,* only this time it's "my" blood and the covenant is "new." What Jesus is doing here on Mount Zion with the Twelve Apostles is every bit as significant as what Moses was doing at Mount Sinai with the Twelve Tribes. The covenant relationship with God is being completely remade.

Jesus says, "This cup is the New Covenant," drawing a straight line back to Jeremiah 31:31, the only place in the entire Old Testament that speaks of a "New Covenant." "What Jeremiah predicted," Jesus is saying, "I am doing right now."

But Jesus continues: "The New Covenant *in my blood,*" in other words, "consisting of my blood." What Jesus says here also applies to his body, which he gave to the Apostles a few verses earlier. The New Covenant consists of his blood and his body, which is his very self. What Isaiah predicted is coming true: the servant of God is *becoming* the covenant itself (Is 42:6).

What Jesus begins at the Last Supper needs to be completed at the cross. At the Last Supper he gives his body and blood in a sacramental form; at the cross, he will give his body and blood physically. At the beginning of the Last Supper, Jesus speaks about "not drinking the fruit of the vine again until the Kingdom of God comes" (Lk 22:18). Many Messianic Jews—that is, Jews who have become Christians and recognize Jesus as the Messiah—notice that the accounts of Jesus's last Passover with the disciples seem incomplete. Usually four cups of wine were drunk at a Passover celebration. In Luke's account of the Last Supper, which is the fullest of any of the gospels, one can only see Jesus drinking the second and third cups of the Jewish Passover ceremony. Then, according to Matthew and Mark, the disciples sing a hymn, after which they should drink the fourth and last cup of wine. But instead, they leave the upper room for the Mount of Olives (Mk 14:26).

Strangely, in the Garden of Gethsemane (which is at the foot of the Mount of Olives), Jesus prays that "this cup may pass from me" (Mk 14:36). Judas shows up with a gang of soldiers. Jesus is arrested, and we all know the rest of the story: his suffering, torture, and trials before the high priest, Herod Agrippa, and Pontius Pilate.

But the idea of the "cup" and the "fruit of the vine" comes back at the cross, where the soldiers offer Jesus a crude form of wine as a pain reliever. The first time Jesus refuses (Mt 27:34), but the second time, both Matthew and John make clear that *he drinks*! (Mt 27:48; Jn 19:29). John's account is best known:

> After this, Jesus, knowing that all was now finished, said (to fulfill the scripture), "I thirst." A bowl full of soured wine stood there; so they put a sponge full of the soured wine on hyssop and held it to his mouth. When Jesus had received the wine, he said, "It is finished"; and he bowed his head and gave up his spirit. (Jn 19:28–30)

"Wait, Jesus, I thought you said you would not drink again of the 'fruit of the vine' *until the kingdom of God comes*!? Did you forget? And what do you mean 'it is finished'? What? What is 'finished'?"

I think that question has more than one answer. Several scholars suggest it means the Passover ceremony: the fourth and last cup, which Jesus never seems to drink at the Last Supper, he now drinks at the cross. It's a theory we may never be able to prove, but I think it is correct. The unbloody gift of himself at the Last Supper is linked to the bloody gift of himself on the cross as one worship ceremony, one liturgical act.

The Passover Jesus begins in the Upper Room is completed at Calvary. Somehow, this seems to be very appropriate.

The fact that Jesus drinks on the cross also indicates that the kingdom of God has arrived. It may not seem like it. In the darkness of Calvary, with Jesus dead and darkness and confusion all around, it does not seem like the dawn of the kingdom of God. Yet we should remember that the creation of the world began in darkness, with the earth empty and formless. It took six days for it to arrive at its full form. Likewise, the dawn of the kingdom of God, the new creation, actually arrives in the darkness and emptiness of Calvary.

The combination of the Upper Room and Calvary gives us the icon for the Eucharistic Covenant. First, I draw Calvary, which is a shape we should be familiar with already:

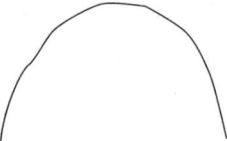

Then we add the Body and Blood on one side . . .

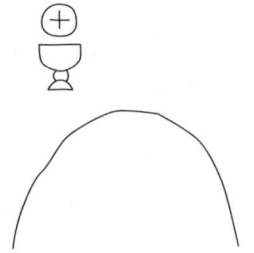

The Eucharistic Covenant

and the cross on the other:

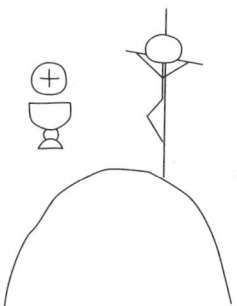

There. Now we have the icon for the Eucharistic Covenant. Really, the Eucharistic Covenant is the same as the New Covenant. However, for the sake of learning salvation history, I like to call it the "New" when it's being prophesied and the "Eucharistic" after its fulfillment.

There's one thing we need to add to the icon, though. St. John reports something rather unusual he saw from the foot of the cross:

> One of the soldiers pierced his side with a spear, and at once there came out blood and water. (Jn 19:34)

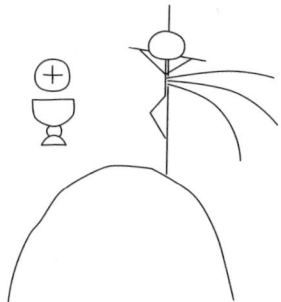

Jews in Jesus's day would have been familiar with a stream of blood and water. During Passover, tens of thousands of lambs were sacrificed in the temple, and the huge amounts of lambs' blood drained out the side of the Temple Mount and down into the brook called the Kidron that ran along the valley below. So Jews visiting Jerusalem at Passover would see a stream of blood and water flowing from the temple.

In John 2, Jesus had said, "Destroy this temple and in three days I will raise it up." His body is the temple, and it is flowing with the blood and water of the Passover. There's more to it, though. The prophet Ezekiel had a famous vision of the new temple of the end times, in which a miraculous river, the river of life, flowed out from it (Ez 47:1–12).

That river of life is nothing other than the Holy Spirit, which flows from the body of Christ. The blood and water from Jesus's body on the cross was not the Holy Spirit itself but rather a *sign* or *symbol* of the living river of the Spirit that was unleashed for us by Jesus's death. For that reason, I usually add the river of the Spirit to the icon:

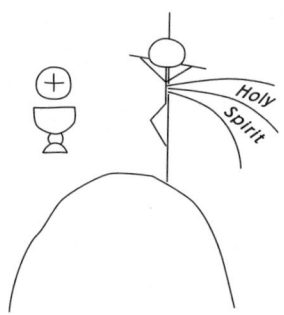

The blood and water from the side of Christ also stand for the sacraments: the Eucharistic blood and the water of baptism. It is through the sacraments that the Spirit comes to us. It is both the river of the Spirit and the river of the sacraments.

The physical flow from Jesus's crucified body was a symbol. The actual pouring out of the Spirit takes place a little later, especially at an event we call Pentecost.

The Eucharistic Covenant

Fifty days after Passover was a feast called "Pentecost," from the Greek word *pentekoste* meaning "fiftieth." In Jesus's day, this feast was also a celebration of the giving of the Law (the Ten Commandments) at Sinai.

Acts 2 tells us that, when the Feast of Pentecost came, all the apostles were again gathered in the Upper Room, the site of the Last Supper. Suddenly, a mighty rushing wind came from heaven and filled the room, and tongues of flame came to rest on the heads of each of the apostles. This was the Holy Spirit, in a visible form.

The wind and the fire remind us of God's appearance on Sinai in wind, fire, and other features of a great storm. But the storm of God at Sinai was frightening; this "storm of the Spirit" at Pentecost is inviting. The wind is mighty but not dangerous; the flame is real but does not hurt or destroy.

Jeremiah promised that, in the New Covenant, the law would be written on the heart. Here, during the celebration of the giving of the Law at Sinai, the Holy Spirit comes down and inhabits the hearts of the first Christians. St. Thomas Aquinas says that the new law of the New Covenant is nothing other than the grace of the Holy Spirit. The Holy Spirit lives in us, teaches us what is right from wrong, and more importantly, gives us the power to do what is right.

The Spirit given to the Apostles at Pentecost also empowers them to speak in other languages. This attracts quite an international crowd from among the Jews who are present in Jerusalem on pilgrimage for this holy day:

> And at this sound the multitude came together, and they were bewildered, because each one heard them speaking in his own language. And they were amazed and wondered, saying, "Are not all these who are speaking Galileans? And how is it that we

hear, each of us in his own native language?" (Acts 2:6–8)

These Jews were from every part of the Roman Empire, from Europe to the border of India. They were confused because they could understand what the apostles were saying. There is a bit of a joke here, a contrast with the ancient account of the Tower of Babel (Gn 11). At Babel, the peoples were confused because they *could not understand* each other's speech. At Pentecost, the crowds are confused because they *can* understand what the apostles are saying! If Babel scattered the human family, Pentecost begins to regather it.

Sensing an excellent opportunity to preach, Peter speaks to the crowds about Jesus and the salvation he offers (Acts 2:14–36). If you look carefully at what Peter actually says, you will see that the theme of his sermon is Davidic Covenant fulfillment: Jesus is the one who fulfills the covenant promises God made to David. Peter can preach this way to the Jews, who know all about the Davidic Covenant and are waiting for its fulfillment. (Later, when the apostles preach to non-Jews, they will have to use a much different approach [Acts 14:15–17].) At the end of Peter's sermon, the crowds of Jews are deeply moved:

> Now when they heard this they were cut to the heart, and said to Peter and the rest of the apostles, "Brethren, what shall we do?" And Peter said to them, "Repent, and be baptized every one of you in the name of Jesus Christ for the forgiveness of your sins; and you shall receive the gift of the Holy Spirit." (Acts 2:37–38)

Notice that Peter urges them to be baptized and connects baptism to the forgiveness of sins and the gift of the Holy Spirit. Baptism is the "sprinkling with clean water" that

Ezekiel predicted when he spoke about the coming "covenant of peace":

> I will sprinkle clean water upon you, and you shall be clean from all your uncleannesses. . . . A new heart I will give you, and a new spirit I will put within you; and I will take out of your flesh the heart of stone and give you a heart of flesh. (Ez 36:25–26)

The fact that the people at Pentecost have been given "a new heart . . . a heart of flesh" can be seen by the fact that they are "cut to the heart." Hearts of stone are not easily cut. Hearts of flesh, however, can be wounded, can be moved.

Ezekiel's "new Spirit" is the Holy Spirit, given along with the waters of baptism, which cleanse all "*uncleanesses*," in other words, *sins*. This is also what Jeremiah said: "I will forgive their iniquity, and I will remember their sin no more" (Jer 31:34).

This is how the crowds respond:

> So those who received his word were baptized, and there were added that day about three thousand souls. And they devoted themselves to the apostles' teaching and fellowship, to the breaking of bread and the prayers. (Acts 2:41–42)

The crowds respond by receiving the sacraments: baptism (v. 41) and Eucharist (v. 42). Verse 42 is actually a description of the early Mass. We continue to do the four actions listed in each Mass: "Devotion to the apostle's teaching" is the Liturgy of the Word, where we listen to the scriptures explained in light of the teaching of the Apostles. "Fellowship" is expressed by the passing of the peace and the collection (the passing of the plate), which shows our unity of love and unity of goods respectively. The "Breaking of the Bread" is St. Luke's early term for the Liturgy of the Eucharist itself. And "the prayers" are the liturgical prayers that fill the Mass from beginning to end.

The sacraments are how the Holy Spirit is given to us. If we look back at St. Peter's sermon, we see him saying things like the following:

> This Jesus God raised up, and of that we all are witnesses. Being therefore exalted at the right hand of God, and having received from the Father the promise of the Holy Spirit, he has poured out this which you see and hear. (Acts 22:32–33)

The crowds could not see Jesus enthroned, but they could observe the effects, which included the outpouring of the Spirit, visible in the tongues of flame, and audible in the rushing wind and different languages of the apostles.

The mental image St. Peter describes is something like this:

The Father is giving the Spirit to Jesus Christ the Son, who is pouring it out on the apostles.

Jesus is completing what was symbolized on the cross, where we saw the river of blood and water flow from his side. We said that was a symbol of the river of life, the Holy Spirit, flowing out from him, in the form of the sacraments: baptism (water), and Eucharist (blood).

Now at Pentecost, the symbolism becomes reality. Jesus is pouring out the Holy Spirit on the Apostles, who preach to the people. The people are persuaded. They receive the sacraments, which communicate the Holy Spirit to them also. They drink from the river of life flowing from the side of Christ.

Baptism is a spiritual rebirth. It's how we become children of God. "To all who received him, who believed in his name, he gave power to become children of God; who were born, not of blood nor of the will of the flesh nor of the will of man, but of God" (Jn 1:12–13). You will hear politicians and public figures say, "We are all God's children." That sounds nice, but it's not quite right. We should say, "We *could* all be God's children." Every human being has the potential to be a child of God. But the potential doesn't become real unless you are baptized. That's the teaching of the Apostles. If there was some other way to become a child of God, then Jesus didn't need to come, suffer, die, and rise from the dead.

With the gift of the Holy Spirit, we have come full circle in salvation history. The *divine filiation* that Adam enjoyed in the Garden—the relationship of sonship to God—has been given back to all human beings. St. Paul says,

> But when the time had fully come, God sent forth his Son, born of woman, born under the Law [i.e., the Mosaic Covenant] to redeem those who were under the Law, so that we might receive adoption as sons. And because you are sons, God has sent

the Spirit of his Son into our hearts, crying, "Abba! Father!" So through God you are no longer a slave but a son, and if a son then an heir. (Gal 4:4–7)

That gives each one of us the Adamic "shine" back:

Our faces beam because we are "children of God." And that's something unique to Christianity. Other religions don't even *claim* to make you a child of God. In Islam, God has no children, just servants—slaves, really. The best you can hope for is to be a good slave. In Buddhism, God may or may not exist; it doesn't really matter because your goal is to lose the illusion of your selfhood, not to become God's child. In Hinduism, God is not a loving Father; God is ultimately an impersonal Force that can take different forms. In most forms of Judaism, God is *like* a Father—but for *Jews* only. And in atheism, you're just another accident in one big accidental universe. The different religions are not paths up the same mountain. They are climbing different mountains:

The Eucharistic Covenant

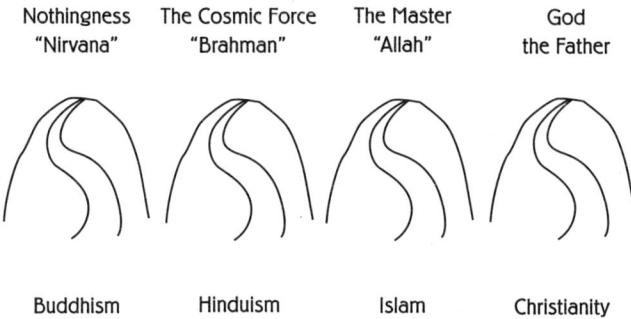

Speaking of mountains . . . we have now made a complete tour of the seven mountains and mediators of salvation history:

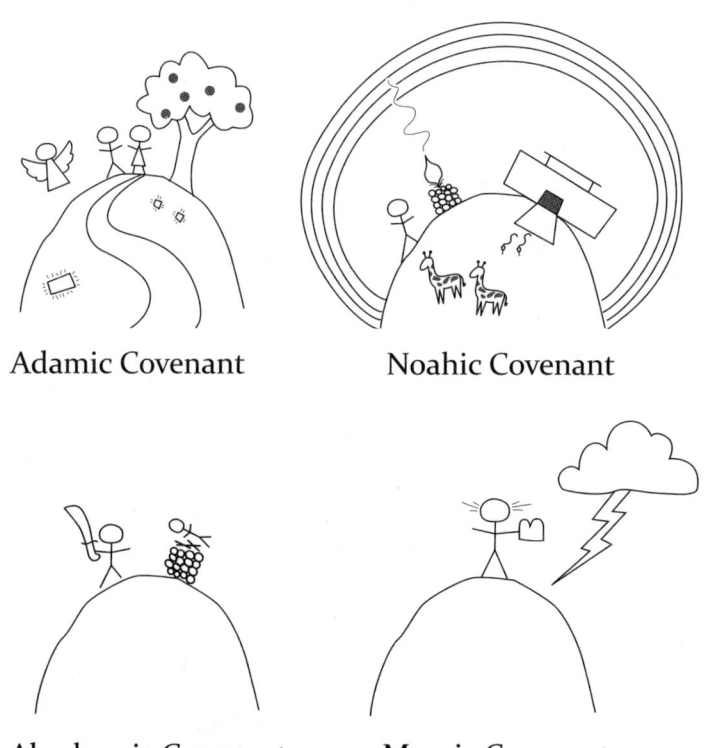

Davidic Covenant

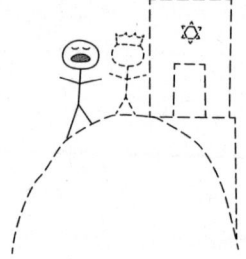
New Covenant

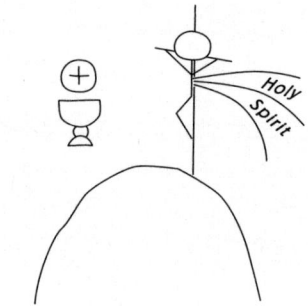
Eucharistic Covenant

SELF-STUDY GUIDE

Background

This chapter teaches about the covenant that fulfills all the Old Testament covenants and is the everlasting covenant for all time, calling it the "Eucharistic Covenant" after its fulfillment. In previous chapters, it was called the "New Covenant" because it was being prophesied, but really the Eucharistic Covenant is the same as the New Covenant. In the Eucharist, the events of salvation become present and actual. Christ's sacrifice on the cross is re-presented—that is, made present again. The Eucharist is a sacrifice because, in it, Christ gives the Church the very Body he gave up on the Cross and the very Blood he "poured out for many for the forgiveness of sins" (Mt 26:28). The Eucharist is offered for the sins of the living and the dead "so that they may be able to enter into the light and peace of Christ" (*CCC*, 1371).

Reading Comprehension

1. What was the problem from a Jewish perspective of the Maccabean kings and King Herod ruling the Jews?

2. What is the importance of the use of *the* in the beginning of Jesus's genealogy in Matthew 1:1: "This is the genealogy of Jesus Christ, *the* son of David, *the* Son of Abraham"?

3. How is Jesus the actual Son of God?

4. Cite one gospel example that makes it clear that Jesus is the King, the Son of David.

5. Explain how the tunic Jesus wore at his crucifixion helps to identify him as priest.
6. How does Jesus fulfill the other roles of Adam (prophet and bridegroom)?
7. Explain two connections between Jesus and Moses.
8. The Davidic Covenant had four basic promises. How did Jesus fulfill the promise that the Son of God would build a better temple than Solomon?
9. What are two major connections of the New (Eucharistic) Covenant with the Old Covenant?
10. How is Jesus's unbloody sacrifice of himself at the Last Supper linked to the bloody gift of himself on the Cross as one worship ceremony, one liturgical act?
11. What do the blood and water from the side of Christ on the Cross stand for?
12. When does the actual pouring out of the Spirit take place?
13. What Old Testament event does the wind of fire of Pentecost remind us of?
14. How do Catholics today receive the gift of the Holy Spirit?
15. A unique aspect of Christianity is that Christians are "children of God." How does this differ from other religions?

The Eucharistic Covenant

Reading in Context

In your notebook, identify the following terms mentioned in this chapter based on the descriptions.

Herod	Pentecost	Pharisees	Abba
Eucharist	Ezra	Babel	Joshua
Maccabees	Passover	Pilate	

1. A prophet who helped the Jews reconstruct their lives after the Babylonian exile
2. A warrior family who expelled King Antiochus IV
3. A descendant of Esau, hence not able to take the throne of David
4. A word Jesus used for "father"
5. A sect of Jews that challenged Jesus for breaking Sabbath laws
6. A man who shared the same Hebrew name with Jesus
7. One of the most important Jewish feasts
8. A man mentioned in our creeds who tried Jesus
9. A Greek word that means "fiftieth"
10. A place mentioned in the Old Testament where people were confused because they couldn't understand each other
11. First known as the "Breaking of the Bread"

Writing Assignment

God's omnipotence—that he is "almighty"—is the only one of St. Thomas Aquinas's attributes of God that is found in the Catholic creeds. Respond to the following question in three to four well-written paragraphs: Do you find the fact that God is almighty more scary or comforting? Explain.

Small-Group Guide

Opening Prayer

Loving Father,

Thank you for this precious gift of your Word, through which we may come to know and worship you more fully and love you more deeply.

Lord Jesus Christ, today we gather as your disciples. We sit at your feet ready to listen to your Word. We humbly ask that you open our ears so that we may hear with our intellect and open our hearts so that we may know you intimately.

Come, Holy Spirit; fill us with your gifts of wisdom, understanding, and knowledge so that we may grow in love, faithfulness, and joy. Amen.

Discussion Questions

1. Since the end of Solomon's reign, we've seen a steady decline of the Jewish nation, both politically and in the faith tradition. Now, at the opening of this chapter, we see a nation that has slowly been recovering its position. It's not quite at the height of its heyday as it was in David's time, but there are signs of it recovering its identity as God's Chosen People.

    List three major events that affected the Jewish nation, and briefly state the consequences of those events.

2. Explain the significance of genealogy to the Jewish people. Identify the lineage of the Maccabees and the Herods. Why were these houses destined to fail? Were they not part of Abraham's legacy? How do you understand where the Abrahamic and Davidic Covenants fit in these scenarios?

3. John Bergsma's illustrations are fun, but they are also excellent tools to visually capture and represent the complexity of the roles and covenants in the biblical narrative. Use Bergsma's illustrations to identify Jesus as the new Adam. Identify the five roles that Jesus fulfills. Discuss these roles in relation to the covenants.

   How does understanding these roles help you understand the person of Jesus better?

4. Connect each of the previous covenants to the Eucharistic Covenant. Relate each major player to Jesus. How is the Eucharistic Covenant the culmination of all the covenants that preceded it?

5. This chapter first explains Jesus as the fulfillment of the earlier covenants and then explains the institution of the Eucharist as the formation of a new and everlasting covenant. What does the "New Covenant" mean to you?

6. Will you respond differently when you hear the words "everlasting covenant" in the Mass?

Bonus: In your notebook, draw a stick figure of yourself, joyful in your role as child of God. Add Jesus beside you.

Closing Prayer

Loving Father,

Thank you for your greatest gift to us, your Son, Our Lord Jesus Christ. We are grateful for your expansive and perfect love.

We praise you and glorify you in word and deed as we strive to love you as you love us.

Bless us in our endeavor to live fully your teachings. Amen.

EIGHT
COVENANT CONSUMMATION
The Wedding Feast of the Lamb

Suggested Reading: Revelation 1, 17, 21-22

In the last chapter, we saw how Jesus established the Eucharistic Covenant by his life, death, and resurrection. We saw how we can once again become children of God by receiving God's Spirit in baptism and renewing that Spirit in us with the Eucharist and other sacraments. And that's what the Christian Church has been doing in the roughly two thousand years since Jesus ascended into heaven. But there's one question we haven't answered yet: Where are we going?

I suppose one answer we could give is "heaven." We know that for each one of us heaven is the goal. Walking with Jesus, strengthened by the sacraments, we hope to see God face-to-face in the life to come after we die physically.

But what about human history? Is God still working in history, guiding it toward some goal? The answer to that is a resounding yes! God has not taken his hands off the steering wheel. We're still on a road trip to a family wedding. Jesus will return, the Church will be purified, and history will end. The Bible describes it as "the Wedding Feast of the Lamb."

The one book of the Bible that speaks the most about the end of history is the Book of Revelation. (Notice that it's singular: Revelation, not Revelations. It's one of the most common confusions!) It's called the Book of Revelation because in it a certain man by the name of John writes down a *revelation* or vision that he had of heaven and the end of time. Tradition tells us this John is the Apostle John, and there are important similarities between the Book of Revelation and the Gospel of John.

Revelation is one of the most controversial books in the Bible—maybe *the* most controversial book. Not every Church Father accepted it. Down through the ages, some Christians have found it frightening and ignored it. Others found it fascinating and obsessed over it. Everyone has found parts of it difficult to understand.

To this day, big arguments are fought over Revelation, and some Christians almost insist that it must be interpreted in a certain way or else a person can't be saved. That's not true, of course. Salvation comes from following Jesus, who said, "If anyone would come after me, let him deny himself, take up his cross daily, and follow me" (Lk 9:23). Salvation doesn't depend on interpreting Revelation exactly right—good thing, too!

In this short chapter, we're not going to solve all the problems of interpreting Revelation. We are, however, going to get its "big picture" of where we are headed in human history.

First, let's get a little overview of the book. Revelation begins with St. John exiled on a barren, little island called Patmos that lies off the coast of modern-day Turkey near the city of Ephesus, an important early Christian center. John doesn't tell us exactly when he is writing, but it may have been in the AD 60s, during the persecution under the infamous emperor Nero. Nero was the one who had Peter and Paul executed in Rome.

It is Sunday morning, and John suddenly finds himself caught up in a vision in which he sees Jesus. Jesus now has a glorious body that reveals his divine power. Our Lord has John write down a message to seven local churches in the main cities of Asia Minor (modern-day Turkey). Jesus has both encouragements and warnings for all these local churches. After John writes down the messages, he is taken further up into heaven and gets a glimpse of the heavenly worship of the saints and angels. In John's visions, the acts of worship in heaven are similar to acts of worship on earth familiar to Jews and Christians:

- incense is offered in prayer;
- bowls of wine are poured out as an offering (*libation* bowls);
- trumpets are blown to praise God and get people's attention; and
- sealed scrolls are broken open and read.

Interestingly, as John watches these things take place in the heavenly worship service, he also sees remarkable events taking place on earth: great plagues, catastrophes, and judgments leading up to the end of history. At the end of all of this, John witnesses the finale: a great and very evil city, portrayed as a harlot, is overthrown by various disasters. Then a new city, portrayed as a bride, comes out of heaven from God. She unites with a figure called "the Lamb." God's people enter the city, and God takes away all their sadness, wounds, and sorrows.

That's the basic plot of the book. Now, what is it talking about? I would suggest two things: (1) the Mass, and (2) human history.

First, Revelation tells us about the Mass. We all know—or should know—that every time we go to Mass we are spiritually joined to the heavenly worship that is going on all the time with the angels and saints in God's presence. That's why, just before the Sanctus, the priest says words such as these: "And so, with all the choirs of angels in heaven we proclaim your glory, and join in their unending hymn of praise." Then we all sing or say, "Holy, holy, holy . . ." as do the angels in Revelation 4:8.

When I was a Protestant pastor, I used to needle Catholics about all the strange ceremonies that took place in Mass: all the robes, candles, censers, and so forth. As with other Protestants, I joked it was all a bunch of "bells and smells" and completely "unbiblical."

Of course, I never asked myself whether the things I used in my own worship service were "biblical": where in the Bible, for example, do you find suits and ties? How about microphones and electric guitars?

Actually, I never realized it but the kinds of clothing and items used in Catholic Mass *are* very biblical. It just didn't occur to me to look in the Book of Revelation. In this book, we see the heavenly models of the things we use in Mass: candlesticks, altars, incense and censers, white robes, bowls, sacred books, and musical instruments. Revelation has served as the inspiration for our worship through the centuries. The Church has modeled her worship after patterns God showed John.

And that's profoundly right because when we go to Mass it is the same worship that is going on in heaven. The same person is at the center: the Lamb of God who takes away the sins of the world (Rv 5:12–13; Jn 1:29). Jesus the Lamb is in heaven,

The Wedding Feast of the Lamb 193

and at the same time, his body and blood is the Eucharist we receive at Mass. He joins us to the angels and saints.

Revelation shows us the reality that is taking place at every Mass and teaches us that our worship is a foretaste of heaven. Now, not everyone might be happy about that. For many, Mass is boring, so if it is a foretaste of heaven, the future life doesn't sound so attractive. Why do we get bored in Mass? We're bored because our bodies don't respond to the reality taking place. We usually don't get physical sensations when we take Jesus's body and blood, soul and divinity into ourselves. We have to trust in faith that it is really happening. On this earth, due to sin, there's a disconnect between reality and our bodies.

In heaven, our glorified bodies will respond to the joy of what is taking place. Husbands and wives know the joy of being joined together as one body with their spouse. So Revelation describes heaven as "the wedding" of the Lamb and his bride. In heaven, we will experience the joy of being joined to Jesus our bridegroom. It will no longer take an act of faith to believe it is happening. It's hard to imagine what it could possibly be like, but St. Paul, who did visit heaven, describes it like this: "No eye has seen, nor ear heard, nor the heart of man conceived, what God has prepared for those who love him" (1 Cor 2:9).

But the Book of Revelation is also about human history. Near the beginning of the book, John greets his Christian readers with a blessing: "Grace to you and peace from him who is and who was and who is to come" (Rv 1:4). In one sense, it is Jesus who "is and was and is to come." Jesus is here in the present ("who is"), in the past ("who was"), and in the future ("who is to come"). The present, past, and future are also three aspects of reading this book: Revelation tells us about the historical work of Jesus in the past ("who was"), the present ("who is"), and the future ("who is to come"). The book works at all three levels.

"Who Was" in the Past

Let's start with the past. Revelation tells us about events that happened long ago during the destruction of the city of Jerusalem in AD 70. When John was writing in the 60s, these events were in the near future ("what must soon take place," 1:1), but now we look at them in hindsight. Much of the Book of Revelation is a buildup to the overthrow of a "great city" described as a "harlot" in league with a terrible "beast" or "dragon" (Rv 17–18). Many think this "great city" and "harlot" is the city of Rome, but Rome was never overthrown the way this city is. However, there was another "great city" that was overthrown in the manner described (17:16) around the time of the writing of the book, and that was Jerusalem. People don't make the connection because they miss these clues: Revelation says the "great city" is where the "lord was crucified" (11:8): obviously Jerusalem. Furthermore, Jerusalem is often called a harlot in the Old Testament (Is 1:21; Jer 2:20; 3:1, 8; Ez 16, 23). In St. John's time, Jerusalem was incredibly wealthy and influential—possibly the wealthiest city in the Roman Empire. The wealth of the city described in Revelation 18 is no exaggeration of Jerusalem.

Revelation 17 says the harlot city relied on a seven-headed beast. This beast probably does represent Rome; the leaders of Jerusalem owed their power to Rome and depended on Rome to maintain their positions. But around AD 66, the relationship with Rome broke down. Jerusalem revolted. The "beast" of Rome then turned on the city and destroyed her. It was one of the greatest human catastrophes in ancient history. The Jewish historian Josephus lived during the destruction of Jerusalem and recorded the events. He puts the numbers of victims in the millions and records that miraculous signs in the heavens—such as described in Revelation—occurred before the destruction of the city. Several scholars have shown how specifics of the plagues and destructions mentioned in Revelation sound strikingly similar to horrific events surrounding the capture of Jerusalem.

Revelation tells us about the past, something that "was." It describes, in symbolic and colorful ways, the plagues and disasters that fell on Jerusalem leading up to the utter destruction of the city by the Roman "beast" (Rv 17–18). The Temple city of Jerusalem was then replaced by a new "Temple city," the Church (Rv 19). The bridal city that descends in Revelation 21 replaces the harlot city destroyed in Revelation 17. This represents the Church being established on earth as the place of worship for God instead of the stone Temple that once stood in Jerusalem.

"Who Is" in the Present

But there's more. Revelation also describes the *present*. Throughout Revelation, we see patterns that repeat themselves in every age, including our own. Revelation tells a story of human rebellion against God that provokes plagues as judgment. But the plagues result not in repentance but rather in further hatred of God. Revelation also tells the story of a harlot city who manipulates world power for her own prosperity and persecutes God's people in order to do it. Yet in the end, that city finds herself destroyed by the very powers she was wielding against God's people. Yes, this is what the Jerusalem establishment was doing in ancient times, but there have been many other cities that have followed the same course at various times: Paris, Rome, Berlin, Moscow, Istanbul, and others. All have, at times, been centers of power and persecution, unleashing hatred on God's people. For a time it seems to go unchecked, but finally, the city collapses. In every age we see harlot cities, bestial empires, and antichrists.

In another book St. John himself says, "You have heard that antichrist is coming, so now many antichrists have come; therefore we know that it is the last hour" (1 Jn 2:18). There have been many antichrists, often political leaders who pose as godsent saviors. They claim to be new messiahs but are in fact demonic tyrants. At times, the conflict between good and evil can truly become "apocalyptic." We can hardly blame many for thinking that the world was coming to an end during the Thirty Years War, the French Revolution, World War I, the Russian Revolution, World War II, and many lesser-known conflicts. All of these were signs of the great final conflict that will precede the coming of Christ.

"Who Is to Come" in the Future

Finally, Revelation does indeed tell us about the future, what "is to come." It describes a series of worldwide plagues and disasters that will fall on the earth before Christ's return and the final judgment. Based on Revelation and other parts of scripture, the Church has always known that there would be a time of testing and trial before the end comes. The *Catechism* puts it this way: "Before Christ's second coming the Church must pass through a final trial that will shake the faith of many believers" (675). "The triumph of Christ's kingdom will not come about without one last assault by the powers of evil" (680). In America, many Christians believe that followers of Jesus will be "raptured" or taken into heaven before the times of testing and trial fall on the earth. That's a pleasant thought, and it's easy to see its appeal. But it's not what the Church has believed or what the scriptures teach. The rapture theory was popularized by a Protestant preacher from Britain named John Nelson Darby in the early 1800s. But Jesus taught

The Wedding Feast of the Lamb

that his disciples would go through the final tribulation (Mt 24:9–14, 20–21).

How can Revelation both describe the destruction of Jerusalem (something in the past) and the end of the world (something in the future)? That's a great question. To understand how and why this can be, we have to know something about Jerusalem, especially the Temple. The Temple of Jerusalem was a symbol of the whole cosmos. It was the "navel of the universe." The garments of the high priest, the liturgical vessels, and the architecture and decoration of the Temple itself were designed to represent the universe and all that was in it: the sun, the moon, the stars, the skies and seas, the earth, plants, animals, angels, and human beings. When the high priest entered the Temple to worship and sacrifice, he was the cosmic man entering the Temple of the Universe to glorify God. The holiness of the Temple spread out to fill the whole city of Jerusalem. It wasn't a city with a Temple: it was a Temple city. Therefore, when the Romans destroyed both Jerusalem and the Temple in AD 70, it had cosmic significance. It was the symbolic destruction of the universe. And the kinds of disasters that fell on Jerusalem before the end are signs and prophecies of what will happen on the whole earth before the end of time.

But we don't want to get stuck on the hard times that will come before the end. God will get us through it! It won't last forever! Instead, we want to focus on the joy that comes afterward. The Bible calls it the "Wedding Feast of the Lamb," and it will literally be the party that ends all parties!

St. John describes the Lamb's wedding feast in the last two chapters of the Bible. In a vision, he saw "the holy city, new Jerusalem, coming down out of heaven from God, prepared as a bride adorned for her husband." This bride is very beautiful, covered with gold and gemstones of every kind (Rv 21:15–21).

However, it would be tough to make a wedding dress to fit her. Some say the ideal dress size would be 36–26–36, but this bride measures about 1,500–1,500–1,500—and that's in miles, not inches! (Rv 21:16). Actually, this bride is a perfect cube, a great rectangular city coming down from heaven to "marry" the lamb. We'll draw her like so:

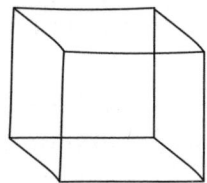

And then we'll add some wings for her to fly down from heaven:

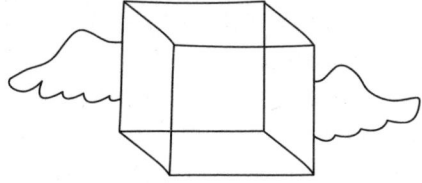

We should explain the meaning of the cube shape. In the Bible, there is only one holy thing that is a perfect cube: the Holy of Holies. The Holy of Holies was the most inner room of the Temple where the Ark rested and God's presence was felt. The cubical shape of the New Jerusalem means that, in the future, the entire people of God will be one big Holy of Holies. God will be just as present in every part of his new Temple city as he once was in the Holy of Holies.

That new Temple city is the Church. St. Paul calls the Church "a holy temple in the Lord" (Eph 2:21) and asks Christians, "Do you not know that your body is a temple of the Holy Spirit?" (1 Cor 6:19).

The bride coming down from heaven is the Church. We know because the Church is called bride, temple, and heavenly Jerusalem in other parts of the New Testament (Eph

2:19–22; 5:25–32; Heb 12:22–24). She comes down to meet her bridegroom, Jesus, who appears as a lamb:

This reminds us of what John the Baptist said when he first saw Jesus: "Behold, the Lamb of God, who takes away the sins of the world!" (Jn 1:29). The lamb is standing on a "great, high mountain," the heavenly Mt. Zion.

We put it all together, and we get our final icon of salvation history: covenant consummation at the Wedding Feast of the Lamb.

Covenant consummation means fulfillment or completion of all the covenants. In the bride, the New Jerusalem, we find images and reminders of all the biblical covenants.

From the center of the city flows the river of life, and the tree of life is growing on both sides of the river (Rv 22:1–2). We have not seen the river and the tree since Eden and the Adamic Covenant. However, we recall that the river of blood and water from the side of Christ's body was an image of the river of life, which is the Holy Spirit.

The city has twelve gates, each with the names of the twelve tribes of Israel. Israel was the grandson of Abraham and heir to the Abrahamic Covenant (Rv 21:12).

The city has twelve foundations, each made from one of the gemstones Moses used to make the breastplate of the high priest (Rv 21:19–20; see Ex 28:17–21), reminding us of the Mosaic Covenant.

The city is called the "holy city Jerusalem." Jerusalem was David's capital, which God chose to be part of the covenant he made with David (Rv 21:10; see Ps 132).

The city has foundations, and on them are written the names of the Twelve Apostles, the very men who first entered the New Covenant with Jesus in the Upper Room (Rv 21:14; see Lk 22:20, 28–30).

So in the bride of the Lamb, the New Jerusalem, all the best of each of the covenants is there.

It's clear that the bride has come for a wedding, and a wedding forms a marriage covenant. So the bride and the Lamb on the heavenly Zion are truly in a covenant relationship. But the word *covenant* does not occur in these last chapters of the Bible. So we're not going to count this eighth icon as another covenant. Why not? First, it's the final form of the Eucharistic Covenant. Second, covenants have a purpose: to make people into a family. Covenant isn't the goal, family is. So in these last chapters of the Bible, we don't hear about covenant anymore, but we do have the language of family. "God himself will be with them, and he will wipe away every tear from their eyes" (Rv 21:3–4) as a good father does for his daughter with a scraped knee. "I will be his God and he shall be my son" (Rv 21:7) God promises to all who persevere through the final test. "They shall see his face, and his name shall be on their foreheads" (Rv 22:4): they will all carry the family name and see their father face-to-face.

So the final vision of human history is God dwelling with his people in their family home, the New Jerusalem. On the one hand, we can say that the New Jerusalem is heaven, and in a sense, that's right. On the other hand, however, we know that the bride of Christ already exists on earth and that the Church is already the Temple city of God. It takes faith to see it because all of us in the Church aren't perfect. In heaven, we will be perfect. So we call the Church in heaven the "Church triumphant." Those in heaven have triumphed over sin, death, and the devil. But here on earth we are the "Church militant" because we are still fighting against those things. Yet even though we're fighting, we remain the bride of Christ and temple of God. So the vision at the end of the Book of Revelation shows us the Church coming to earth as the true temple of God to replace the stone Temple in Jerusalem destroyed by the Romans. That happened in the past (AD 70). But it's also a vision of the future, when sin, death, and the devil will be no more and all God's people will live with him as children with a father.

There's no vision more beautiful. The Bible does not end with the final freeze-up of the universe ("heat death"), with the end of the cycles of reincarnation, or even with a divine master handing out rewards to his servants. The Bible ends with the people of God "wedded" to Jesus the Lamb and living in a great city that is their family home where their Father God lives close to them. That's what we have to look forward to!

SELF-STUDY GUIDE

Background

This chapter is an overview of the Book of Revelation. It does not cover an eighth covenant. The word "covenant" does not occur in this last book of the Bible. Yet Revelation describes a wedding in which the bride (Christ) has come for the bridegroom (his Church). This is the final form of the Eucharistic Covenant. In this last book of the Bible, "covenant" is never mentioned, but the language of family is. God will care for his people as loving human parents care for their own children. The book uses symbolic and an apocalyptic style of writing to describe events of the past, present, and future. The visions of the Book of Revelation herald our destiny to be wedded to Jesus the Lamb and living in the great eternal city with our families and with God himself.

Reading Comprehension

1. Who is the author of the Book of Revelation, and what is its setting?
2. How are the acts of heavenly worship described in Revelation the same as earthly worship?
3. How is Revelation connected with the Mass?
4. What three aspects of human history are present in the Book of Revelation?
5. What city was the "great city" and "harlot" Revelation describes? What city was the "seven-headed beast"? How did the relationship between these two cities end?

6. Name two of the antichrists that have plagued the world and are mentioned in this chapter.
7. Why was Rome's destruction of the Jerusalem Temple in AD 70 a symbolic destruction of the universe?
8. What is the significance of describing as a cube the bride that comes down from heaven to marry the lamb?

Reading in Context

In your notebook, match each of the terms used in this chapter with its definition below.

Nero	harlot	raptured	cosmos
Holy of Holies	seven-headed beast	Sanctus	Asia Minor
Church militant	Church triumphant	Patmos	

1. Thought to be a reference to ancient Rome in the Book of Revelation
2. Modern-day Turkey
3. The Church on earth
4. The sum of everything
5. To be transported to heaven at the time of the second coming
6. A word that means "Holy" and describes a part of the Mass
7. An infamous Roman emperor who ordered Peter and Paul to be executed

8. The island where the vision in the Book of Revelation was received
9. The inner room of the Temple where the Ark of the Covenant rested
10. Thought to be a reference to Jerusalem in the Book of Revelation
11. The Church in heaven

Writing Assignment

Revelation 21–22 beautifully describes the heavenly city that awaits all Christians who endure suffering in this life. Their constant prayer—"Come, Lord Jesus"—is answered now and will be answered always. Read the two chapters in Revelation and then answer in complete sentences the following questions:

- Why is there no need for a temple in the new city?
- What is your own image of heaven compared to Revelation's poetic image?

Small-Group Guide

Opening Prayer

Loving Father,

Thank you for this precious gift of your Word, through which we may come to know and worship you more fully and love you more deeply.

Lord Jesus Christ, today we gather as your disciples. We sit at your feet ready to listen to your Word. We humbly ask that you open our ears so that we may hear with our intellect and open our hearts so that we may know you intimately.

Come, Holy Spirit; fill us with your gifts of wisdom, understanding, and knowledge so that we may grow in love, faithfulness, and joy. Amen.

Discussion Questions

1. What are the three time periods referenced in Revelation? How does breaking down this complex book of the Bible into these distinct eras help you see Revelation in a broader sense and give it historical relevance as well as a modern perspective?

2. Describe the "new Temple city" (page 198). Consider the historical meanings of temple, both literal and figurative.

3. Analyze the Bride and the Lamb. What and whom do these characterizations symbolize?

4. The beautiful imagery of family completes the relationship we began as children of God. Explain the metaphor of the Wedding Feast of the Lamb. Are we invited to this feast as neighbors or family?

5. How does this symbolism of the Bride and the Lamb change or support your understanding of Revelation? Of your faith? Of your understanding of the Catholic Church?

Bonus: In your notebook, draw a stick figure of yourself, joyful in your role as child of God. Place yourself in heaven, surrounded by God's love.

Closing Prayer

Eternal Father,

Thank you for the gift of the Holy Mass, which gives us a foretaste of heaven. We are grateful for the celebration of the Eucharist.

We praise you and glorify you in word and deed as we strive to one day join you in heaven.

Bless us in our endeavor to live fully your teachings. Amen.

A Last Word

We've made a whirlwind tour of the biblical story line. I hope you have found it helpful.

The *Catechism of the Catholic Church* says that the most important principle for interpreting the Bible is to keep in mind "its content and unity" (112).

You've already had some exposure to the "content" of the Bible just by listening at Mass and reading the Bible occasionally on your own. The main goal of this book was to show the Bible's "unity"—how it all fits together. One of the prayers at Mass used to say, "Again and again you offered a covenant to man, and through the prophets taught him to hope for salvation." We saw how true that prayer was as we examined the sequence of covenants throughout salvation history beginning with Adam and ending with Jesus.

My hope is that this book has provided a "big picture" that will help make more sense of the smaller "portraits"—the selections from the Bible that we hear in Mass or read on our own. With the visual "horizon" of the mountains and mediators in your mind's eye, it's possible to fit most of the stories and teachings of the Old Testament into their proper place in the story line. It's also possible to hear the gospel readings with greater appreciation as we see in Jesus's words and actions reminders of Adam, Moses, David, and other great covenant mediators.

We begin to have the déjà vu feeling that the gospel authors wanted us to experience when we listen to the life of Jesus.

At the end of this book, we can now make a summary of the message of the Bible: the sonship Adam once enjoyed with God has been restored to us by Jesus Christ. Just as God breathed the "breath of life" into the nostrils of Adam and made him a living being, so through baptism Jesus shares with us the "Spirit of Life," the Holy Spirit that makes us living children of God.

What's the appropriate response to the message of scripture?

First, *we can receive the sacraments with greater enthusiasm.* We now have an idea of the "big story" of salvation history. A good story leaves you with the desire to take part in it: for example, my sons were enthralled with the *Star Wars* movie series and spent large amounts of their allowances buying *Star Wars* figures and gadgets that let them reenact the story line. But the Bible is much better than science fiction. It is, as the saying goes, "The Greatest Story Ever Told." It's natural that we should want to *take part* in it, and God has provided a way through the sacraments.

The sacraments make us participate in the events of scripture. When we are baptized, we experience

- creation emerging from the waters at the dawn of time;
- the family of Noah surviving the waters of the flood;
- the Israelites crossing the Red Sea; and
- Jesus sinking and rising in the Jordan River at the hands of John the Baptist.

Through the power of the sacraments, we share in all those experiences, and our story becomes part of The Greatest Story.

Likewise, when we receive the Eucharist, we are sharing in

- the fruit of the Tree of Life in the Garden of Eden;
- the manna from heaven during Israel's wanderings in the wilderness;
- the great feasts held by David and his successors in Jerusalem; and
- the last Passover supper of Jesus and his apostles.

All those events become things that *we* have done, and the story of scripture becomes *our* story. This is the sacramental mystery.

Second, *we can live our Catholic faith with more zest.* Our faith teaches us that, as children of God through Christ, all the rights and privileges of Adam have been restored to us. Like Adam, we can call God "Father" (Lk 3:38). As royalty, we rule over our passions and possessions, rather than being ruled *by* them. As prophets, we speak God's word to the people around us. As priests, we offer to God our very lives on a daily basis, as a "living sacrifice" for the salvation of the whole world. Finally, as grooms and brides, we find our love and joy in embracing our true Spouse every time we come forward to receive communion. As we seek to live out these roles, we can benefit from some excellent guidance the *Catechism* provides on living out our share of Christ's kingship (908), priesthood (901), prophetic office (904–907), and enjoying him as our spiritual Spouse (796, 1821).

Third, *we can keep learning more of God's Word.* If you've never read through the Bible before, maybe it's time to give it a try. There are several excellent plans for reading through the Catholic Bible in one, two, or three years. I suggest one such plan in the "Suggestions for Further Reading" section, and there are many others free for download on the internet. While you read through scripture, you will probably want to have handy a more substantial textbook on the Bible that goes into greater detail than we were able to in these few pages. Again, I offer several possibilities in "Suggestions for Further Reading."

Fourth, *we can share what we know.* This book has been short, our words have been basic, and the artwork was simple. Nonetheless, I believe the concepts we have shared and the symbols we've used can be a powerful way to remember and convey some profound concepts about God's plan through history.

We shouldn't be too proud to use simple symbols to communicate. The cross is a very simple symbol, yet it packs more theological punch than we could discuss in twenty books.

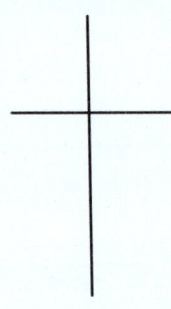

You don't have to have a degree in scripture to share what you know. You can use the sketches you've learned to share some basic Bible concepts to a catechism class, a youth group, a Bible study, a friend, or your spouse. Some of my students have done the seven covenants on felt banners or PowerPoint slides or transformed them into a semester's worth of youth group lesssons. Go ahead, feel free to share!

Notes

Introduction

page 1   "quote one of the popes saying"
At least two popes have made statements similar to this. Leo XIII, in the encyclical *Providentissimus Deus,* calls the scriptures "a Letter, written by our heavenly Father, and transmitted by the sacred writers to the human race in its pilgrimage so far from its heavenly country" (1). Pius XII, in his encyclical *Divino Afflante Spiritu,* says, "It behooves us to be grateful to the God of all providence, Who from the throne of His majesty has sent these books as so many paternal letters to His own children" (19).

page 1   "Ignorance of Scripture"
This famous excerpt from Jerome's *Commentary on Isaiah* (Nn. 1.2: CCL 73, 1–3) is used in the Office of Readings for the Feast of St. Jerome on September 30.

page 2   "I began to see the unity of the Bible"
Some scholarly works that helped me understand the covenant pattern in scripture include Scott W. Hahn, *Kinship by Covenant: A Canonical Approach*

to the Fulfillment of God's Saving Promises (New Haven, CT: Yale University Press, 2009); Paul R. Williamson, *Sealed with an Oath: Covenant in God's Unfolding Purpose* (Downers Grove, IL: InterVarsity Press, 2007); Gorden P. Hugenberger, *Marriage as Covenant: Biblical Law and Ethics as Developed from Malachi* (Grand Rapids, MI: Baker Academic, 1994). There is a convergence between Catholic, Protestant, and Jewish thinkers, as well as between modern critics and the Church Fathers, that *covenant* provides the organizing scheme of the Old Testament. For example, contemporary Jewish biblical critic R. E. Friedman writes: "The E text pictured a covenant between God and Israel at Sinai, the J account added an Abrahamic covenant, the Josianic Deuteronomistic Historian developed the Davidic covenant, and the Priestly narrative added a covenant with Noah. These four primary covenants, the Noahic, Abrahamic, Mosaic, and Davidic, provided a narrative framework in which legal, historical, legendary, poetic, and so on, materials could meet" ("The Hiding of the Face: An Essay on the Literary Unity of Biblical Narrative," in *Judaic Perspectives on Ancient Israel* [eds. J. Neusner et al.; Philadelphia: Fortress, 1987], 214). On the other hand, the Church Father Irenaeus notes: "For this reason were four principal (lit. "catholic"!) covenants given to the human race: one, prior to the deluge, under Adam; the second, that after the deluge, under Noah; the third, the giving of the law, under Moses; the fourth, that which renovates man, and sums up all things in itself by means of the Gospel, raising and bearing men upon its wings into the heavenly kingdom"

(*Against Heresies*, bk. III, ch. 11, 8). See also the *Catechism*, 70–73, and Walther Eichrodt, *Theology of the Old Testament*, vol. 1 (Philadelphia: Westminster/John Knox Press, 1961).

page 3   "One of the Eucharistic Prayers"
This is from the Thanksgiving of the Fourth Eucharistic Prayer, which used to be translated, "Again and again you offered a covenant to man, and through the prophets taught him to hope for salvation." The new translation reads, "Time and again you offered them covenants and through the prophets taught them to look forward to salvation."

page 4   "Source and Summit of the Christian life"
John Paul II emphasized this truth throughout his ministry, especially in his encyclical *Ecclesia de Eucharistia* ("The Church of the Eucharist," see 1). The actual statement is a quote of the Second Vatican Council, the Dogmatic Constitution on the Church *Lumen Gentium*, 11.

page 4   "*a legal way to make someone part of your family*"
My preferred definition is "the extension of kinship by oath." For technical studies on the nature of covenant, see Frank Moore Cross, "Kinship and Covenant in Ancient Israel," in *From Epic to Canon: History and Literature in Ancient Israel* (Baltimore: Johns Hopkins University Press, 1998), 1–8; Gordon Hugenberger, *Marriage as a Covenant: A Study of Biblical Law and Ethics Governing Marriage, Developed From the Perspective of Malachi* (Leiden, Netherlands: Brill, 1994), esp. 197; and Scott Hahn, *Kinship by Covenant:*

A Canonical Approach to the Fulfillment of God's Saving Promises, Yale Anchor Bible Reference Library (New Haven, CT: Yale University Press, 2009), 28–31, 37–39, and throughout.

page 5   "Relationships are casual"
Although not written from a Christian perspective, sociologist Kathleen Bogle documents the commitment-free attitude toward intimate relationships on American college campuses in *Hooking Up: Sex, Dating, and Relationships on Campus* (New York: NYU Press, 2008). This campus culture almost never serves the best interests of young women.

1: Setting the Son in the Garden

page 11   "People naturally want to ask"
The exact relationship between the creation account in the Bible and the scientific account of the origin of the universe has been discussed at least since the time of the fathers. St. Augustine believed creation took place instantaneously, and the six-day pattern of Genesis 1 was an accommodation to created intellects. For magisterial teaching on the issue, see Pope Pius XII's encyclical *Humani Generis*. For a treatment of the issues involved, see Pope Benedict XVI, *"In the Beginning": A Catholic Understanding of the Story of the Creation and the Fall* (Grand Rapids, MI: Eerdmans, 1995). Another good treatment from a Christian, although not specifically Catholic, perspective is Henri Blocher's *In the Beginning: The Opening Chapters of Genesis* (Downers Grove, IL: InterVarsity, 1984). For a defense of a more literal-historical reading of the creation account

from a Catholic perspective, see Father Victor P. Warkulwiz, M.S.S., *The Doctrines of Genesis 1–11: A Compendium and Defense of Traditional Catholic Theology on Origins* (Caryville, TN: John Paul II Institute of Christian Spirituality, 2007).

page 19 "The language of creation resembles the language of Moses building the Tabernacle in the wilderness"
See G. K. Beale, *The Temple and the Church's Mission: A Biblical Theology of the Dwelling Place of God* (Downers Grove, IL: InterVarsity, 2004), 60–61; Scott Hahn, *A Father Who Keeps His Promises* (Ann Arbor, MI: Servant Publications, 1998), 51–53.

page 19 "Some scriptures speak of the creation as a temple"
See Beale, *The Temple and the Church's Mission*, 29–50. Beale states, "The Old Testament temple was a microcosm of the entire heaven and earth. . . . The Psalmist [Ps 78:69] is saying that . . . God designed Israel's earthly temple to be comparable to the heavens and the earth" (31–32).

page 19 "people considered the whole universe a kind of temple"
See Beale, *The Temple and the Church's Mission*, 50–52: "It is now widely known that archaeological ruins and texts from the Ancient Near East portray ancient temples as small models of heavenly temples or of the universe conceived of as a temple" (51).

page 21   "For the ancient reader, Adam's commission to 'serve and guard' in the garden would have had a priestly sound to it"
See Beale, *The Temple and the Church's Mission*, 66–70: "When . . . these two words . . . occur together in the Old Testament, they refer either to Israelites 'serving' God and 'guarding [keeping]' God's word . . . or to priests who 'keep' the 'service' . . . of the tabernacle" (67; see Nm 3:7–8, 8:25–26, 18:5–6; 1 Chr 23:32; Ez 44:14).

page 21   "Later temples were decorated to look like it"
See Lawrence E. Stager, "Jerusalem and the Garden of Eden," *Eretz Israel* 26 (Festschrift F.M. Cross; Jerusalem: Israel Exploration Society), 183–189.

page 21   "The ancient Jews took this for granted"
See Beale, *The Temple and the Church's Mission*, 70.

page 23   "How shall we denote Adam as a prophet?"
The idea of Adam as a prophet may be supported by the fact that the vast majority of the uses of the term "Son of Adam" (Hebrew *Ben-Adam*) in the Old Testament refer to the *prophet* Ezekiel (Ez 2:1 and 92 other times in the Book of Ezekiel). Ezekiel is also the biblical author with the most to say about Eden (Ez 27:23; 28:13; 31:9,16,18; 36:35).

page 23   "he becomes The Bard"
Some may not catch my joke here: Shakespeare is known as "The Bard," and he wrote poetry in iambic pentameter, a certain kind of rythmic writing

style. The idea is, upon seeing the woman, Adam becomes a poet.

page 24 "this elegant little statement of Adam's . . . is covenant-making language"
See Walter Brueggemann, "Of the Same Flesh and Bone," *Catholic Bible Quarterly* 32 (1970): 532–42.

page 29 "Some key features of the Adamic or Creation Covenant"
Not all scholars agree that there is a covenant between God and Adam, but Jewish and Catholic traditions have generally favored this view. Hosea 6:7 (in the Hebrew) and Sirach 14:17 give canonical support to the presence of a covenant with Adam, and this concept is reflected in liturgical texts: "When your bride, deceived by the evil one, broke faith with you, you did not abandon her. With everlasting love you renewed with your servant the covenant you made with Adam" (from the "Consecration of the Professed [Women Religious]," No. 72 of the *Roman Ritual*). The presence of a covenant from the beginning of creation was affirmed by St. John Paul II (*Redemptor Hominis*, 7) and Pope Benedict XVI ("*In the Beginning*," 27). Some contemporary interpreters also defend a creation or Adamic Covenant: see Craig Bartholomew, "Covenant and Creation: Covenant Overload or Covenant Deconstruction?" *Calvin Theological Journal* 30 (1995): 11–33, esp. 28–30.

page 30   "ancient readers knew that Eden was the model for temple building"
See Beale, *The Temple and the Church's Mission*, 72 n.101; and Lawrence E. Stager, "Jerusalem and the Garden of Eden," *Eretz Israel* 26 (Festschrift F.M. Cross; Jerusalem: Israel Exploration Society, 1999), 183–189.

2: Washing Up and Starting Over

page 37   "Snakes are almost never a good thing in the Old Testament"
On the ancient symbolism of snakes, see Richard E. Averbeck, "Ancient Near Eastern Mythography as It Relates to Historiography in the Hebrew Bible: Genesis 3 and the Cosmic Battle," in *The Future of Biblical Archeology* (Grand Rapids, MI: Eerdmans, 2004), 328–56.

page 39   "the ancient Israelite temple had only one entrance, facing east"
See Beale, *The Temple and the Church's Mission*, 74.

page 40   "People have puzzled over who is meant by the 'Sons of God' since ancient times"
The apocryphal *Book of Jubilees*, a Jewish religious writing from the second century BC, presents the "Sons of God" as fallen angels, as does *1 Enoch* and other Jewish writings from this time period found among the Dead Sea Scrolls.

page 44   "a renewal of the covenant with Adam"
See the "Consecration of the Professed (Women Religious)," No. 72 of the *Roman Ritual*, and William J. Dumbrell, *The Faith of Israel: Its*

Expression in the Books of the Old Testament (Grand Rapids, MI: Baker, 1988), 21–22.

3: A New Hope

pages 51–52 "There are possible answers to all these questions"
See John Bergsma and Scott Hahn, "Noah's Nakedness and the Curse on Canaan (Gn 9:20–27)," *Journal of Biblical Literature* 124, no. 1 (2005): 25–40.

page 52 "The Babel story is kind of a parallel to the Sons of God–Daughters of Men account"
See Gary A. Rendsburg, *The Redaction of Genesis* (Winona Lake, IN: Eisenbrauns, 1996), 19–22.

page 54 "there are three specific things God promises to Abram"
See Hahn, *Kinship by Covenant*, 103.

page 57 "When people would cut up animals and walk between them"
See Jeremiah 34:12–20, and Hugenberger, *Marriage as a Covenant*, 209–10.

page 57 "what scholars call *divine condescension*"
There is an excellent book on this subject: S. D. Benin, *The Footprints of God: Divine Accommodation in Jewish and Christian Thought* (Albany, NY: SUNY, 1993).

page 59 "In ancient times, the term 'great name' was connected to kings"
See Moshe Weinfeld, *The Promise of the Land: The Inheritance of the Land of Canaan by the*

Israelites (Berkeley: University of California Press, 1993), 261.

page 59   "Furthermore, kings were known as 'fathers' of their countries"
See Weinfeld, *The Promise of the Land*, 248, and sources cited.

page 60   "This was because covenant-making ceremonies usually involved cutting something"
See, again, Jeremiah 34:12–20 and Hugenberger, *Marriage as a Covenant*, 193–96.

page 62   "we can be sure that Isaac has fully cooperated"
The Jewish tradition is reflected in the ancient historian Josephus, in *Antiquities of the Jews*, 1:226 (public domain editions are available online); and the apocryphal 4 Maccabees 13:12, 18:3. See, further, Géza Vermès, "Redemption and Genesis XXII," in *Scripture and Tradition in Judaism. Haggadic Studies* (Leiden, Netherlands: Brill, 1961), 193–227.

page 62   "a death he freely accepted"
This phrase is from the old translation of Eucharistic Prayer II, now rendered he "entered willingly into his Passion."

page 62   "The phrase 'only begotten'"
See Gerhad Kittel, ed., *Theological Dictionary of the New Testament* (Grand Rapids, MI: Eerdmans, 1967), 4:737–41.

page 65   "Throughout the Bible, 'swearing an oath' and 'making a covenant' mean almost the same thing" See Hugenberger, *Marriage as a Covenant*, 182–85.

page 67   "The Jewish tradition concluded that the killing of animals, by itself, could not have meant much to God"
The statements in this paragraph are based on the study of the Targums, the ancient translations of the Old Testament into Aramaic, the spoken language of the Jews in postexilic Israel. The Targums not only translated but also amplified and interpreted the biblical text, revealing the common understanding of scripture among Jews of Jesus's day. On the significance of the Akedah in the Targums, see Robert Hayward, *Divine Name and Presence: The Memra* (Totowa, NJ: Allanheld, Osmun, 1981), 96–106; and Hahn, *Kinship by Covenant*, 128–29 and sources cited. Hayward states, "It is the 'Akedah which validates the sacrifices offered in the Temple to atone for sins; it is the 'Akedah which merits the Passover; and it is through the 'Akedah that God remembers Israel, hears and answers their prayers, forgives their sins, and rescues them from afflictions" (96).

4: God's Laws, Israel's Flaws

page 74   "The Israelites ended up as slaves of the Egyptians"
On the historicity of the Exodus, see James K. Hoffmeier, *Israel in Egypt: The Evidence for the Authenticity of the Exodus Tradition* (Oxford: Oxford University Press, 1999).

page 75	"We know of other examples of people doing this in ancient times"
	Besides Moses, the best-known historical character who was floated down a river was Sargon of Akkad, a Mesopotamian king whose dates are given as 2270 to 2215 BC.
page 76	"As expected, the sand blows off"
	There is no specific ancient tradition that the sand blew off the victim's body, but it is a plausible scenario.
page 77	"In a mysterious way, the name expressed the *reality* of the person"
	Rabbi Berel Wein, an Israeli-American authority on Jewish law and theology, states it this way: "In our name lies our soul and self."
page 77	"rather a word that probably meant 'HE IS'"
	Although one cannot be certain, the form YHWH appears to be an archaic third masculine singular imperfect form of the Hebrew verb *HYH*, "to be." See Francis Brown, *The New Brown, Driver, Briggs, Gesenius Hebrew and English Lexicon* (1907; reprint Peabody, MA: Hendrickson, 1979), 217–18.
page 78	"that word 'serve' in Hebrew is often used of *worship*"
	See Brown, *Lexicon*, 712–13 (definitions 4 and 5).

Notes to Chapter Four

page 79   "The ten plagues were contests between the Lord, God of the slaves, and the gods of the Egyptians"
See Exodus 12:12, Numbers 33:4, and John Currid, *Ancient Egypt and the Old Testament* (Grand Rapids, MI: Baker Academic, 1997), 108–13.

page 81   "you shall be to me a *royal priesthood*"
Most English translations render this as "kingdom of priests, " but the Hebrew can also be rendered "royal priesthood" as it is in the ancient Greek translation (called the Septuagint) and the New Testament (1 Pt 2:9). For a modern defense of this translation, see John Davies, *A Royal Priesthood: Literary and Intertextual Perspectives on an Image of Israel in Exodus 19.6* (London: T&T Clark International, 2004).

page 83   "two beams of light coming from his face"
St. Jerome mistranslated the Hebrew verb *qaran,* "send forth rays, shine," as "grow horns" in Exodus 34:35—an easy mistake, since the verb *qaran* is related to the noun *qeren,* "horn." See Brown, *Lexicon,* 901–2.

page 86   "decorated with reminders of Eden"
See Beale, *The Temple and the Church's Mission,* 66–80.

page 87   "bull worship, like they had done in Egypt"
The golden bull calf probably represented the Egyptian god Apis. See Moshe Weinfeld, *Deuteronomy 1–11,* Anchor Yale Bible 5 (New York: Doubleday, 1991; reprint, New Haven, CT: Yale University Press, 1995), 424.

page 88 "Christians have viewed these additional laws . . . as having a *penitential purpose*"
This view is reflected in the important ancient Christian document *Didascalia Apostolorum* (The Teaching of the Apostles), possibly composed in the second or third century AD: *The Didascalia Apostolorum in Syriac, Vol. II: Chapters XI–XXVI*, trans. A. Vööbus, CSCO 408, Scriptores Syri 180 (Leuven, Belgium: Secretariat du CSCO, 1979), 243–44. See also St. Thomas Aquinas's treatment of the Old Law in *Summa Theologica* Part 1, Part 2, Questions 98–105, esp. Q. 101, art. 3, *reply*: "Many obligations had to be laid on these men [the Israelite], so that, with all the burdens involved in the worship of God, they should have no time for idolatry"; and also Q. 102, art. 3, *reply*: "Thus a further reason may be given for the sacrificial ceremonies, namely that they withdrew men from offering sacrifices to idols. That is why the precepts about sacrifice were not given to the Jews till after they had fallen into idolatry in adoring the golden calf; the sacrifices being instituted so that the people, in their proneness to offer sacrifice, might do so to God rather than idols." Also relevant to the concept of penitential laws is the study by Stephen D. Benin, *The Footprints of God: Divine Accomodation in Jewish and Christian Thought* (Albany: SUNY Press, 1993).

pages 88–89 "They were meant to teach certain spiritual truths"
This is a consensus of both the Christian and the Jewish tradition, affirmed in the treatments of the Mosaic Law in both St. Thomas Aquinas's *Summa Theologiae* and Moses Maimonides' *The Guide for the Perplexed*.

page 90 — "at least nine rebellions against God recounted in the Book of Numbers"
By my count, these rebellions are: (1) Nm 11:1–3, (2) 11:4–35, (3) 12:1–16, (4) 14:1–38, (5) 14:39–45, (6) 16:1–35, (7) 16:41–50, (8) 20:1–13, (9) 25:1–15.

page 93 — "some of the laws Moses gives in Deuteronomy weren't God's best laws"
On this whole subject, see Hahn, *Kinship by Covenant*, 73–77, and sources cited therein.

5: Once and Future King

page 106 — "Eight is sometimes considered the biblical number of a new beginning"
The eighth day is also the first day of the next week, thus it represents the beginning of a new cycle. Eight was considered the number of a new beginning and also of the transcendent in later Jewish mystical traditions, but we can't be sure it held this significance for all the biblical authors.

page 108 — "He also introduced singing and music into worship for the first time"
Many scholars, following the great Israeli thinker Yehezkel Kaufmann, believe the Mosaic liturgy was celebrated in silence. See Israel Knohl, *The Sanctuary of Silence: The Priestly Torah and the Holiness School* (Minneapolis, MN: Fortress Press, 1994). Knohl's book is not directly about the practice of the Mosaic liturgy but takes its title from the idea that ancient Israelite worship took place in silence. David's introduction of music in the liturgy is recorded in 1 Chronicles 15–16.

page 109 "From another perspective, we might say David was so important in the Bible because God made a very special covenant with him"
See the lengthy treatment in Hahn, *Kinship by Covenant*, 176–213.

page 110 "a strong connection between the Abrahamic Covenant and the Davidic Covenant"
See Hahn, *Kinship by Covenant*, 117–23.

page 114 "Who was Melchizedek?"
For the connection between Salem and Jerusalem, see Psalm 76:2; Josephus, *Antiquities of the Jews*, 1:180; and Jon D. Levenson, *The Death and Resurrection of the Beloved Son* (New Haven, CT: Yale University Press, 1995), 121. For a discussion of Melchizedek, see Hahn, *Kinship by Covenant*, 189–93, 299.

page 114 "All the rights and privileges of Melchizedek fell to David"
H-J Kraus, *The Theology of the Psalms* (Minneapolis, MN: Augsburg 1986), 115: "The Davidic king entered into the ancient functions of the Jebusite royal city-state, whose founder was Melchizedek."

page 115 "many of the Psalms of David are not only worship songs but prophecies"
See, for example, Acts 2:29–31 and the great Psalms scroll among the Dead Sea Scrolls "11QPsalms[a]," which ends with the summary statement: "All these he [David] uttered through prophecy which was given him from before the Most High." (11QPs[a] col. 27; see Geza Vermes, *The*

Dead Sea Scrolls in English [2nd Ed.; New York: Penguin Books, 1984], 265.)

page 116   "the only two places in the Bible where the phrase 'bone and flesh'"
On this phrase, see Walter Brueggemann, "Of the Same Flesh and Bone," *Catholic Biblical Quarterly* 32 (1970): 532–42. Brueggemann argues that the key phrase in 2 Samuel 5:1 "clearly is a *covenant formula*, an oath of abiding loyalty, one that expresses communal solidarity through covenant more than blood kinship by birth" (535; emphasis mine).

6: Stormy Today, Sonny Tomorrow

page 127   "The flowers, animals, gold, and jewels called to mind Eden and the Adamic Covenant"
See Beale, *The Temple and the Church's Mission*, 66–80.

page 127   "scholars have pointed out intentional similarities in the way the Ark and the Temple were built"
Compare the three levels of the Ark (Gn 6:16) and the three levels of the Temple (1 Kgs 6:6; Ez 41:6). See also Lawrence E. Stager, "Jerusalem and the Garden of Eden," *Eretz Israel* 26 (Festschrift F.M. Cross; Jerusalem: Israel Exploration Society), 183–189. The Ark may be thought of as a floating "zoological garden," a microcosm of the biological world, and therefore a buoyant Eden.

page 127   "later Jewish tradition holds"
See last note on chapter 3.

page 128   "the son of David, heir of David's covenant, will be responsible to make sure that Israel follows the Mosaic Covenant"
This is why, in subsequent biblical history, the fate of the nation is tied so closely to the covenant fidelity (or infidelity) of the king. Compare the perspective of 2 Kings 17:21–23.

page 129   "they returned to the worship of golden calves"
Compare Exodus 32:4, 8 with 1 Kings 12:28.

page 133   "God's special Servant, who is the same person as the Son of David mentioned in Isaiah 9 and 11"
Many Bible scholars would not recognize the "servant" of Isaiah as the same person as the "Son of David" in Isaiah 9 and 11. However, as Christians, we know that, in God's providence, Jesus Christ has become the fulfillment of both of these prophetic characters. Furthermore, there are sound exegetical reasons for identifying the "servant" of the second half of the book of Isaiah (Is 40–66) as the Davidic king: see D. I. Block, "My Servant David: Ancient Israel's Vision of the Messiah," in *Israel's Messiah in the Bible and the Dead Sea Scrolls*, ed. R. S. Hess and M. D. Carroll R., 17–56 (Grand Rapids, MI: Baker, 2003), 49–56; and M. L. Strauss, *The Davidic Messiah in Luke–Acts: The Promise and Its Fulfillment in Lukan Christology* (Sheffield, UK: Sheffield Academic, 1995), 292–98.

page 133   "It refers to *covenant love*"
There are numerous studies on the word *hesed*. One of the classics is Nelson Glueck, *Hesed in the Bible*, trans. A. Gottschalk, ed. E. Epstein

(Cincinnati, OH: Hebrew Union College Press, 1967), esp. 55: "*hesed* constitutes the essence of a covenant."

page 137 "For these and other reasons, the rabbis almost didn't allow his book into the Jewish Bible"
The problems the rabbis had with Ezekiel are mentioned in the Babylonian Talmud, Tractate *Sabbath* 13b; and the Mishnah, Tractate *Hagigah* 2:1. See also Daniel I. Block, *The Book of Ezekiel, Chapters 1–24* (Grand Rapids, MI: Eerdmans, 1997), 44.

page 140 "resurrection will also be a part of the new situation in the latter days"
It is often stated by scholars that Ezekiel's vision has nothing to do with actual personal resurrection, but see the discussion in Daniel I. Block, *The Book of Ezekiel, Chapters 25–48* (Grand Rapids, MI: Eerdmans, 1998), 383–92.

7: The Grand Finale

page 153 "He wasn't even a true Jew"
The Jewish historian Josephus mentions this: see his *Antiquities of the Jews,* 14:403 (14.15.2.403).

page 155 "Jesus even calls God his 'Abba'"
See Scott Hahn, ed. *The Catholic Bible Dictionary* (New York: Doubleday, 2009), 5.

page 157 "The implication is that Jesus himself is a priest and has priestly rights"
See Pope Benedict XVI, *Jesus of Nazareth: From the Baptism in the Jordan to the Transfiguration* (New York: Doubleday, 2007), 108.

page 157   "the robe of the High Priest was woven without seams"
See the historian Josephus, in *Antiquities of the Jews*, 3:159–61: "The high priest is indeed adorned with . . . a vestment of a blue color. This also is a long robe, reaching to his feet. . . . Now this vesture *was not composed of two pieces, nor was it sewed together upon the shoulders and the sides, but it was one long vestment so woven as to have an aperture for the neck*" (emphasis mine).

page 164   "We could write a whole book comparing Moses and Jesus"
Many have been written. The best is Dale Allison, *The New Moses: A Matthean Typology* (Minneapolis, MN: Augsburg, 1993).

page 165   "A traditional way of understanding the two different genealogies"
See my entry "genealogy" in *The Westminster Dictionary of New Testament and Early Christian Literature and Rhetoric*, ed. David Aune (Louisville, KY: Westminster John Knox, 2003). Genealogies in the ancient world could be constructed on the basis of legality, biology, or both. In my view, Matthew reveals a concern to establish Jesus as legal heir to the throne in Matthew 1, whereas Luke shows more concern for the person of Mary and the Lord's physical relatives in Luke 1–2. St. Joseph could be considered the son of two men (compare Mt 1:16 with Lk 3:23) because, if the tradition is accurate that the Blessed Virgin was an only child, Joseph would have become the legal son and heir of her father (perhaps "Heli" of Lk 3:23) upon his marriage to her.

page 168   "Usually four cups of wine were drunk at a Passover celebration"
On this, see Brant Pitre, *Jesus and the Jewish Roots of the Eucharist* (New York: Doubleday, 2011), 147–70.

page 172   "huge amounts of lambs' blood drained out the side of the Temple Mount"
The presence of these blood drains in the Herodian Temple is recorded in the *Mishnah*, Tractate *Middoth* 3:2: "And at the south-western corner there were two holes like two narrow nostrils by which the blood that was poured over the western base and the southern base used to run down and mingle in the water-channel and flow out into the brook Kidron" (594).

page 173   "St. Thomas Aquinas says that the new law of the New Covenant is nothing other than the grace of the Holy Spirit"
See, for example, the *Summa Theologica*, parts I–II, Q. 106, art. 1.

8: Covenant Consummation

page 190   "Tradition tells us this John is the Apostle John"
The Greek style of the Book of Revelation is very different from the Gospel of John. Therefore, many scholars do not think they could have been written by the same person. On the other hand, authors' styles change as they age and undergo different life circumstances. If the Book of Revelation was written earlier in John's life (AD 60s) and the Gospel later (AD 90s), John's style may have changed a great deal in those thirty years. For a discussion of the authorship of Revelation,

see *The Ignatius Catholic Study Bible: New Testament* (San Francisco: Ignatius Press, 2010), 489–91; Juan Chapa, *Why John Is Different: Unique Insights in the Gospel and Writings of St. John* (New Rochelle, NY: Scepter, 2013), 214–216; and Michael Barber, *Coming Soon: Unlocking the Book of Revelation and Applying Its Lessons Today* (Steubenville, OH: Emmaus Road, 2005), 1–7, but especially 289–292.

page 191   "it may have been in the AD 60s, during the persecution under the infamous emperor Nero" Revelation is usually thought to have been written either in the 90s under the persecution of the emperor Domitian or in the 60s under the persecution of Nero. Lately, support for the earlier date has been growing, in part because there is no evidence of a persecution under Domitian outside of the Book of Revelation itself. See discussion in Barber, *Coming Soon*, 1–7, 289–292.

page 194   "Revelation tells us about events that happened long ago during the destruction of the city of Jerusalem in AD 70"
Many commentators have thought that the harlot city in Revelation 17 is a picture of Rome, or some extreme Protestants regard it as the Roman Catholic Church. However, others have pointed out strong reasons to identify the harlot city as Jerusalem. See the discussion in the *Ignatius Catholic Study Bible*, 514–515.

page 194 "The wealth of the city described in Revelation 18 is no exaggeration of Jerusalem"
According to the Jewish historian Josephus, the Romans considered Jerusalem wealthier than Rome itself. See Josephus, *Jewish War*, Book VI, 6:2. This has been confirmed by recent archeological analysis that found high concentrations of silver in Jerusalem pottery from this time period that due to the large amounts of silver coinage circulating in the city. See "Silver Anomalies Found in Jerusalem Pottery Hint at Wealth During Second Temple Period," Berkely Lab Research News press release, September 27, 2006 (http://www2.lbl.gov/Science-Articles/Archive/EETD-Jerusalem-pottery.html).

page 194 "The Jewish historian Josephus . . . recorded the events"
See Josephus's work *The Jewish War*, especially Books V and VI. The numbers of casualties are given in Book VI, 9:3. The similarities between the events leading to the destruction of Jerusalem and the narrative of the Book of Revelation have been pointed out by several scholars: for example, Kenneth L. Gentry, *Before Jerusalem Fell: Dating the Book of Revelation* (Atlanta: American Vision, 1998).

page 196 "The rapture theory was popularized by a Protestant preacher from Britain named John Nelson Darby"
See Carl Olson, *Will Catholics Be "Left Behind"?* (San Francisco: Ignatius Press, 2003); and David Currie, *Rapture: The End-Times Error that Leaves*

the Bible Behind (Manchester, MA: Sophia Institute Press, 2004).

page 197   "The Temple of Jerusalem was a symbol of the whole cosmos"
See Josephus, *Antiquities of the Jews*, Book 3:180: "For if anyone do but consider the fabric of the tabernacle, and take a view of the garments of the high priest, and of those vessels which we make use of in our sacred ministration, he will find . . . they were every one made in way of imitation and representation of the universe." Likewise the ancient Jewish philosopher Philo, *Life of Moses*, 2:143: "Then [Moses] gave [the priests] their sacred vestments, giving to his brother [Aaron, the High Priest] the robe which reached down to his feet, and the mantle which covered his shoulders, as a sort of breast-plate, being an embroidered robe, adorned with all kinds of figures, and a representation of the universe."

Compare also *Life of Moses*, 2:135; and Wisdom of Solomon 18:24. See also G. K. Beale, "Cosmic Symbolism of Temples in the Old Testament," 29–80 of idem, *The Temple and the Church's Mission: A Biblical Theology of the Dwelling Place of God* (Downers Grove, IL: InterVarsity Press, 2004); and Jon D. Levenson, *Sinai & Zion: An Entry into the Jewish Bible* (Minneapolis: Winston Press, 1985), 138–39: "The Temple . . . is a microcosm of which the world itself is the macrocosm."

Suggestions for Further Reading

Gray, Tim, and Jeff Cavins. *Walking with God: A Journey Through the Bible.* West Chester, PA: Ascension Press, 2010.

A superb overview of content and structure of the Bible, as well as the proper Catholic approach to interpretation.

Hahn, Scott. *A Father Who Keeps His Promises* (Cincinnati: Servant Books, 1998).

A similar but more substantial overview of salvation history.

Hahn, Scott, ed. *Understanding the Scriptures: A Complete Course in Bible Study.* Didache Series. Chicago: Midwest Theological Forum, 2005.

Written as a high school text, this fine book is also excellent for personal reading. Using a covenant structure very similar to *Catholic Bible Basics,* it delves into the scriptures at much greater depth.

Rojas, Carmen. *How to Read the Bible Every Day: A Guide for Catholics: A One-Year, Two-Year, and Three-Year Plan for Reading Through the Scriptures.* Cincinnati: Servant Books, 1988.

This booklet contains charts of Bible reading plans to help you read through the scriptures at the pace you choose.

Sri, Edward. *The Bible Compass: A Catholic's Guide to Navigating the Bible.* West Chester, PA: Ascension Press, 2009.

Dr. Sri deals clearly with important theological background issues that guide how we interpret the Bible.

John Bergsma is a professor of theology at Franciscan University of Steubenville and vice president for biblical theology and mission effectiveness at the St. Paul Center for Biblical Theology. He served as a Protestant pastor for four years before entering the Catholic Church in 2001 while pursuing a doctorate specializing in the Old Testament and the Dead Sea Scrolls from the University of Notre Dame.

In addition to teaching scripture at Franciscan University, Bergsma is a frequent guest on Catholic radio and speaks regularly at conferences and parishes nationally and internationally. Bergsma has published a number of academic and popular works on the Bible and the Catholic faith, including *Bible Basics for Catholics, New Testament Basics for Catholics, Psalm Basics for Catholics,* and *Love Basics for Catholics.*

He and his wife, Dawn, live with their children in Steubenville, Ohio.

Website: www.johnbergsma.com

Scott Hahn is a popular Catholic theologian, author, speaker, and apologist who founded the St. Paul Center for Biblical Theology and teaches at Franciscan University of Steubenville.

ALSO BY
DR. JOHN BERSGMA

New Testament Basics for Catholics

In *New Testament Basics for Catholics*, Dr. John Bergsma uses simple illustrations and a clear, conversational style to introduce four of the most important writers in the New Testament: Matthew, Luke, Paul, and John.

Psalm Basics for Catholics
Seeing Salvation History in a New Way

In *Psalm Basics for Catholics*, Dr. John Bersgma highlights the presence of Jesus in the psalms and helps us understand their meaning in light of the story of salvation to bridge the gap between the world of contemporary Catholics and the ancient word of the Bible.

Love Basics for Catholics
Illustrating God's Love for Us throughout the Bible

Using his popular, whimsical stick-figure illustrations and engaging style, Dr. John Bergsma helps us understand scripture and salvation history in a unique, memorable way by showing how marriage in the Bible represents the love between God and his people.

Look for the titles in this series wherever books and eBooks are sold.
Visit avemariapress.com for more information.

WANT TO TAKE A COURSE WITH DR. BERGSMA?

Go beyond the basics with Dr. John Bergsma as he guides you through all eight chapters, offering rich pastoral insights and compelling anecdotes you won't find anywhere else.

With his signature blend of scholarly depth, dry wit, and engaging storytelling, Dr. Bergsma will challenge you to consider:
"How do these truths transform my daily life?"

Discover how Scripture can reshape your relationship with God and the world around you.

Purchase access to this video course at **avemariaprapress.com**.